Management Concepts and Organizational Behaviour

INTRODUCTION TO MANAGEMENT

INTRODUCTION TO MANAGEMENT

Objective: The objectives of this lesson are to enable to define management; to describe the nature and scope of management; to know the difference between management and administration; to understand various levels of management; and to describe the various skills that are necessary for successful managers.

Lesson Structure:

1.1 Introduction
1.2 Definition of Management
1.3 Characteristics of Management
1.4 Management Functions/ the Process of Management
1.5 Nature of Management
1.6 Management Vs. Administration
1.7 Levels of Management
1.8 Managerial Skills
1.9 The Manager and his job
1.10 Principles of Management
1.11 Significance of Management
1.12 Summary
1.13 Self Assessment Questions
1.14 Suggested Readings

1.1 INTRODUCTION

A business develops in course of time with complexities. With increasing complexities managing the business has become a difficult task. The need of existence of management has increased tremendously. Management is essential not only for business concerns but also for banks, schools, colleges, hospitals, hotels, religious bodies, charitable trusts etc. Every business unit has some objectives of its own. These objectives can be achieved with the coordinated efforts of several personnel. The work of a number of persons are properly co-ordinated to achieve the objectives through the process of management is not a matter of pressing a button, pulling a lever, issuing orders, scanning profit and loss statements, promulgating rules and regulations. Rather it is the power to determine what shall happen to the personalities and happiness of entire people, the power to shape the destiny of a nation and of all the nations which make up the world." Peter F. Drucker has stated in his famous book "The Practice of Management" that, "the emergence of management as an essential, a distinct and leading social institution is a pivotal event in social history. Rarely in human history has a new institution proved indispensable so quickly and even less often as a new institution arrived with so little opposition, so little disturbance and so little controversy?"

Management is a vital aspect of the economic life of man, which is an organised group activity. It is considered as the indispensable institution in the modern social organization marked by scientific thought and technological innovations. One or the other form of management is essential wherever human efforts are to be undertaken collectively to satisfy wants through some productive activity, occupation or profession.

It is management that regulates man's productive activities through coordinated use of material resources. Without the leadership provided by management, the resources of production remain resources and never become production.

Management is the integrating force in all organized activity. Whenever two or more people work together to attain a common objective, they have to coordinate their activities. They also have to organize and utilize their resources in such a way as to optimize the results. Not only in business enterprises where costs and revenues can be ascertained accurately and objectively but also in service organizations such as government, hospitals, schools, clubs, etc., scarce resources including men, machines, materials and money have to be integrated in a productive relationship, and utilized efficiently towards the achievement of their gals. Thus, management is not unique to business organizations but common to all kinds of social organizations.

Management has achieved an enviable importance in recent times. We are all intimately associated with many kinds of organizations, the most omnipresent being the government, the school and the hospital. In fact, more and more of major social tasks are being organized on an institution basis. Medical care, education, recreation, irrigation, lighting, sanitation, etc., which typically used to be the concern of the individual or the family, are now the domain of large organizations. Although, organizations other than business do not speak of management, they all need management. It is the specific organ of all kinds of organizations since they all need to utilize their limited resources most efficiently and effectively for the achievement of their goals. It is the most vital forces in the successful performance of all kinds of organized social activities.

Importance of management for the development of underdeveloped economies has been recognized during the last one and a half decade. There is a significant gap between the management effectiveness in developed and underdeveloped countries. It is rightly held that development is the function not only of capital, physical and material resources, but also of their optimum utilization. Effective management can produce not only more outputs of goods and services with given resources, but also expand them through better use of science and technology. A higher rate of economic growth can be attained in our country through more efficient and effective management of our business and other social organizations, even with existing physical and financial resources. That is why it is now being increasingly recognized that underdeveloped countries are indeed somewhat inadequately managed countries.

The emergence of management in modern times may be regarded as a significant development as the advancement of modern technology. It has made possible organization of economic activity in giant organizations like the Steel Authority of India and the Life Insurance Corporation of India. It is largely through the achievements of modern management that western countries have reached the stage of mass consumption societies, and it is largely through more effective management of our economic and social institutions that we can improve the quality of life of our people. It is the achievements of business management that hold the hope for the huge masses in the third world countries that they can banish poverty and achieve for themselves decent standards of living.

1.2 DEFINITION OF MANAGEMENT

Although management as a discipline is more than 80 years old, there is no common agreement among its experts and practitioners about its precise definition. In fact, this is so in case of all social sciences like psychology, sociology, anthropology, economics, political science etc. As a result of unprecedented and breath-taking technological developments, business organizations have grown in size and complexity, causing consequential changes in the practice of management. Changes in management styles and practices have led to changes in management thought. Moreover, management being interdisciplinary in nature has undergone changes because of the developments in behavioural sciences, quantitative techniques, engineering and technology, etc. Since it deals with the production and distribution of goods and services, dynamism of its environments such as social, cultural and religious values, consumers' tastes and preferences, education and information explosion, democratization of governments, etc., have also led to changes in its theory and practice. Yet, a definition of management is necessary for its teaching and research, and also for improvement in its practice.

Many management experts have tried to define management. But, no definition of management has been universally accepted. Let us discuss some of the leading definitions of management:

Peter F. Drucker defines, "management is an organ; organs can be described and defined only through their functions".

According to Terry, "Management is not people; it is an activity like walking, reading, swimming or running. People who perform Management can be designated as members, members of Management or executive leaders."

Ralph C. Davis has defined Management as, "Management is the function of executive leadership anywhere."

According to Mc Farland, "Management is defined for conceptual, theoretical and analytical purposes as that process by which managers create, direct, maintain and operate purposive organization through systematic, co-ordinated co-operative human effort."

Henry Fayol, "To mange is to forecast and plan, to organize, to compound, to co-ordinate and to control."

Harold Koontz says, "Management is the art of getting things done through and within formally organized group."

William Spriegal, "Management is that function of an enterprise which concerns itself with direction and control of the various activities to attain business objectives. Management is essentially an executive function; it deals with the active direction of the human effort."

Kimball and Kimball, "Management embraces all duties and functions that pertain to the initiation of an enterprise, its financing, the establishment of all major policies, the provision of all necessary equipment, the outlining of the general form of organization under which the enterprise is to operate and the selection of the principal officers."

Sir Charles Reynold, "Management is the process of getting things done through the agency of a community. The functions of management are the handling of community with a view of fulfilling the purposes for which it exists."

E.F.L. Brech, "Management is concerned with seeing that the job gets done, its tasks all centre on planning and guiding the operations that are going on in the enterprise."

Koontz and O'Donnel, "Management is the creation and maintenance of an internal environment in an enterprise where individuals, working in groups, can perform efficiently and effectively toward the attainment of group goals. It is the art of getting the work done through and with people in formally organized groups."

James Lundy, "Management is principally a task of planning, co-ordinating, motivating and controlling the efforts of other towards a specific objective. It involves the combining of the traditional factors of production land, labour, capital in an optimum manner, paying due attention, of course, to the particular goals of the organization."

Wheeler, "Management is centered in the administrators or managers of the firm who integrate men, material and money into an effective operating limit."

J.N. Schulze, "Management is the force which leads guides and directs an organization in the accomplishment of a pre-determined object."

Oliver Scheldon, "Management proper is the function in industry concerned in the execution of policy, within the limits set up by the administration and the employment of the organization for the particular objectives set before it."

Keith and Gubellini, "Management is the force that integrates men and physical plant into an effective operating unit."

Newman, Summer and Warren, "The job of Management is to make co-operative endeavour to function properly. A manager is one who gets things done by working with people and other resources in order to reach an objective."

G.E. Milward, "Management is the process and the agency through which the execution of policy is planned and supervised."

Ordway Tead, "Management is the process and agency which directs and guides the operations of an organization in the realizing of established aims."

Mary Parker Follett defines management as the "art of getting things done through people". This definition calls attention to the fundamental difference between a manager and other personnel of an organization. A manager is one who contributes to the organization's goals indirectly by directing the efforts of others – not by performing the task himself. On the other hand, a person who is not a manager makes his contribution to the organization's goals directly by performing the task himself.

Sometimes, however, a person in an organization may play both these roles simultaneously. For example, a sales manager is performing a managerial role when he is directing his sales force to meet the organization's goals, but when he himself is contacting a large customer and negotiating a deal, he is performing a non-managerial role. In the former role, he is directing the efforts of others and is contributing to the organization's goals indirectly; in the latter role, he is directly utilizing his skills as a salesman to meet the organization's objectives.

A somewhat more elaborate definition of management is given by George R. Terry. He defines management as a process "consisting of planning, organizing, actuating and controlling, performed to determine and accomplish the objectives by the use of people and other resources". According to this definition, management is a process – a systematic way of doing things. The four management activities included in this process are: planning, organizing, actuating and controlling. Planing means that managers think of their actions in advance. Organizing means that managers coordinate the human and material resources of the organization. Actuating means that managers motivate and direct subordinates. Controlling means that managers attempt to ensure that there is no deviation from the norm or plan. If some part of their organization is on the wrong track, managers take action to remedy the situation.

To conclude, we can say that various definitions of management do not run contrary to one another. Management is the sum-total of all those activities that (i) determine objectives, plans, policies and programmes; (ii) secure men, material, machinery cheaply (iii) put all these resources into operations through sound organization (iv) direct and motivate the men at work, (v) supervises and control their performance and (iv) provide maximum prosperity and happiness for both employer and employees and public at large.

1.3 CHARACTERISTICS OF MANAGEMENT

Management is a distinct activity having the following salient features:

1. **Economic Resource :** Management is one of the factors of production together with land, labour and capital. As

industrialization increases, the need for managers also increases. Efficient management is the most critical input in the success of any organized group activity as it is the force which assembles and integrates other factors of production, namely, labour, capital and materials. Inputs of labour, capital and materials do not by themselves ensure production, they require the catalyst of management to produce goods and services required by the society. Thus, management is an essential ingredient of an organization.

2. **Goal Oriented :** Management is a purposeful activity. It coordinates the efforts of workers to achieve the goals of the organization. The success of management is measured by the extent to which the organizational goals are achieved. It is imperative that the organizational goals must be well-defined and properly understood by the management at various levels.

3. **Distinct Process :** Management is a distinct process consisting of such functions as planning, organizing, staffing, directing and controlling. These functions are so interwoven that it is not possible to lay down exactly the sequence of various functions or their relative significance.

4. **Integrative Force :** The essence of management is integration of human and other resources to achieve the desired objectives. All these resources are made available to those who manage. Managers apply knowledge, experience and management principles for getting the results from the workers by the use of non-human resources. Managers also seek to harmonize the individuals' goals with the organizational goals for the smooth working of the organization.

5. **System of Authority :** Management as a team of managers represents a system of authority, a hierarchy of command and control. Managers at different levels possess varying degree of authority. Generally, as we move down in the managerial hierarchy, the degree of authority gets gradually reduced. Authority enables the managers to perform their functions effectively.

6. **Multi-disciplinary Subject :** Management has grown as a field of study (i.e. discipline) taking the help of so many other disciplines such as engineering, anthropology, sociology and psychology. Much of the management literature is the result of the association of these disciplines. For instance, productivity orientation drew its inspiration from industrial engineering and human relations orientation from psychology. Similarly, sociology and operations research have also contributed to the development of management science.

7. **Universal Application :** Management is universal in character. The principles and techniques of management are equally applicable in the fields of business, education, military, government and hospital. Henri Fayol suggested that principles of management would apply more or less in every situation. The principles are working guidelines which are flexible and capable of adaptation to every organization where the efforts of human beings are to be coordinated.

1.4 MANAGEMENT FUNCTIONS /PROCESS OF MANAGEMENT

There is enough disagreement among management writers on the classification of managerial functions. Newman and Summer recognize only four functions, namely, organizing, planning, leading and controlling.

Henri Fayol identifies five functions of management, viz. planning, organizing, commanding, coordinating and controlling. Luther Gulick states seven such functions under the catch word "POSDCORB' which stands for planning, organizing, staffing, directing, coordinating, reporting and budgeting. Warren Haynes and Joseph Massie classify management functions into decision-making, organizing, staffing, planning, controlling, communicating and directing. Koontz and O'Donnell divide these functions into planning organizing, staffing, directing and controlling.

For our purpose, we shall designate the following six as the functions of a manager: planning, organizing, staffing, directing, coordinating and controlling.

1. **Planning :** Planning is the most fundamental and the most pervasive of all management functions. If people working in groups have to perform effectively, they should know in advance what is to be done, what activities they have to perform in order to do what is to be done, and when it is to be done. Planning is concerned with 'what', 'how, and 'when' of performance. It is deciding in the present about the future objectives and the courses of action for their achievement. It thus involves:

    (a)　determination of long and short-range objectives;

    (b)　development of strategies and courses of actions to be followed for the achievement of these objectives; and

    (c)　formulation of policies, procedures, and rules, etc., for the implementation of strategies, and plans.

    The organizational objectives are set by top management in the context of its basic purpose and mission, environmental factors, business forecasts, and available and potential resources. These objectives are both long-range as well as short-range. They are divided into divisional, departmental, sectional and individual objectives or goals. This is followed by the development of strategies and courses of action to be followed at various levels of management and in various segments of the organization. Policies, procedures and rules provide the framework of decision making, and the method and order for the making and implementation of these decisions.

Every manager performs all these planning functions, or contributes to their performance. In some organizations, particularly those which are traditionally managed and the small ones, planning are often not done deliberately and systematically but it is still done. The plans may be in the minds of their managers rather than explicitly and precisely spelt out: they may be fuzzy rather than clear but they are always there. Planning is thus the most basic function of management. It is performed in all kinds of organizations by all managers at all levels of hierarchy.

2. **Organizing** : Organizing involves identification of activities required for the achievement of enterprise objectives and implementation of plans; grouping of activities into jobs; assignment of these jobs and activities to departments and individuals; delegation of responsibility and authority for performance, and provision for vertical and horizontal coordination of activities. Every manager has to decide what activities have to be undertaken in his department or section for the achievement of the goals entrusted to him. Having identified the activities, he has to group identical or similar activities in order to make jobs, assign these jobs or groups of activities to his subordinates, delegate authority to them so as to enable them to make decisions and initiate action for undertaking these activities, and provide for coordination between himself and

his subordinates, and among his subordinates. Organizing thus involves the following sub-functions :

(a) Identification of activities required for the achievement of objectives and implementation of plans.

(b) Grouping the activities so as to create self-contained jobs.

(c) Assignment of jobs to employees.

(d) Delegation of authority so as to enable them to perform their jobs and to command the resources needed for their performance.

(e) Establishment of a network of coordinating relationships.

Organizing process results in a structure of the organization. It comprises organizational positions, accompanying tasks and responsibilities, and a network of roles and authority-responsibility relationships.

Organizing is thus the basic process of combining and integrating human, physical and financial resources in productive interrelationships for the achievement of enterprise objectives. It aims at combining employees and interrelated tasks in an orderly manner so that organizational work is performed in a coordinated manner, and all efforts and activities pull together in the direction of organizational goals.

3. **Staffing :** Staffing is a continuous and vital function of management. After the objectives have been determined, strategies, policies, programmes, procedures and rules formulated for their achievement, activities for the implementation of strategies, policies, programmes, etc. identified and grouped into jobs, the next logical step in the

management process is to procure suitable personnel for manning the jobs. Since the efficiency and effectiveness of an organization significantly depends on the quality of its personnel and since it is one of the primary functions of management to achieve qualified and trained people to fill various positions, staffing has been recognized as a distinct function of management. It comprises several sub-functions :

(a) Manpower planning involving determination of the number and the kind of personnel required.

(b) Recruitment for attracting adequate number of potential employees to seek jobs in the enterprise.

(c) Selection of the most suitable persons for the jobs under consideration.

(d) Placement, induction and orientation.

(e) Transfers, promotions, termination and layoff.

(f) Training and development of employees.

As the importance of human factor in organizational effectiveness is being increasingly recognized, staffing is gaining acceptance as a distinct function of management. It need hardly any emphasize that no organization can ever be better than its people, and managers must perform the staffing function with as much concern as any other function.

4. **Directing :** Directing is the function of leading the employees to perform efficiently, and contribute their optimum to the achievement of organizational objectives. Jobs assigned to subordinates have to be explained and clarified, they have to be provided guidance in job performance and they are to be motivated to contribute their

optimum performance with zeal and enthusiasm. The function of directing thus involves the following sub-functions :

(a) Communication

(b) Motivation

(c) Leadership

5. **Coordination :** Coordinating is the function of establishing such relationships among various parts of the organization that they all together pull in the direction of organizational objectives. It is thus the process of tying together all the organizational decisions, operations, activities and efforts so as to achieve unity of action for the accomplishment of organizational objectives.

The significance of the coordinating process has been aptly highlighted by Mary Parker Follet. The manager, in her view, should ensure that he has an organization "with all its parts coordinated, so moving together in their closely knit and adjusting activities, so linking, interlocking and interrelation, that they make a working unit, which is not a congeries of separate pieces, but what I have called a functional whole or integrative unity". Coordination, as a management function, involves the following sub-functions:

(a) Clear definition of authority-responsibility relationships

(b) Unity of direction

(c) Unity of command

(d) Effective communication

(e) Effective leadership

6. **Controlling :** Controlling is the function of ensuring that the divisional, departmental, sectional and individual performances are consistent with the predetermined objectives and goals. Deviations from objectives and plans have to be identified and investigated, and correction action taken. Deviations from plans and objectives provide feedback to managers, and all other management processes including planning, organizing, staffing, directing and coordinating are continuously reviewed and modified, where necessary.

   Controlling implies that objectives, goals and standards of performance exist and are known to employees and their superiors. It also implies a flexible and dynamic organization which will permit changes in objectives, plans, programmes, strategies, policies, organizational design, staffing policies and practices, leadership style, communication system, etc., for it is not uncommon that employees failure to achieve predetermined standards is due to defects or shortcomings in any one or more of the above dimensions of management.

   Thus, controlling involves the following process :

   (a) Measurement of performance against predetermined goals.

   (b) Identification of deviations from these goals.

   (c) Corrective action to rectify deviations.

   It may be pointed out that although management functions have been discussed in a particular sequence-planning, organizing, staffing, directing, coordinating and controlling – they are not performed in a sequential order. Management is an integral process and it is difficult to put its functions neatly in separate boxes. Management functions tend to coalesce, and it sometimes becomes difficult to separate one from the other. For example, when a production manager is discussing work problems with one of his subordinates, it is difficult to say whether he is guiding, developing or communicating, or doing all these things simultaneously. Moreover, managers often perform more than one function simultaneously.

1.5 NATURE OF MANAGEMENT

Management has been conceptualized earlier in this lesson, as the social process by which managers of an enterprise integrate and coordinate its resources for the achievement of common, explicit goals. It has developed into a body of knowledge and a separate identifiable discipline during the past six decades. Practice of management as an art is, of course, as old as the organized human effort for the achievement of common goals. Management has also acquired several characteristics of profession during recent times. Large and medium-sized enterprise in India and elsewhere are managed by professional managers – managers who have little or no share in the ownership of the enterprise and look upon management as a career. The nature of management as a science, as art and as a profession is discussed below :

Management as a Science : Development of management as a science is of recent origin, even though its practice is ages old. Fredrick W. Taylor was the first manager-theorist who made significant contributions to the development of management as a science. He used the scientific methods of analysis, observation and experimentation in the management of production function. A perceptive manager, as he was, he distilled certain fundamental principles and propounded the theory and principles of scientific management. His work was followed by many others including Gantt, Emerson, Fayol, Barnard, etc. During the last few decades, great strides have been made in the development of management as a systematized body of knowledge which can be learnt, taught and researched. It has also provided powerful tools of analysis, prediction and control to practicing managers. The scientific character of management has been particularly strengthened by management scientists who have developed mathematical models of decision making.

Another characteristic of science in management is that it uses the scientific methods of observation, experimentation and laboratory research. Management principles are firmly based on observed phenomena, and systematic classification and analysis of data. These analyses and study of observed phenomena are used for inferring cause-effect relationships between two or more variables. Generalizations about these relationships result in hypotheses. The hypotheses when tested and found to be true are called principles. These principles when applied to practical situations help the practitioner in describing and analyzing problems, solving problems and predicting the results.

Even though management is a science so far as to possess a systematized body of knowledge and uses scientific methods of research, it is not an exact science like natural sciences. This is simply because management is a social science, and deals with the behaviour of people in organization. Behaviour of people is much more complex and variable than the behaviour of inanimate things such as light or heat. This makes controlled experiments very difficult. As a result, management principles lack the rigour and exactitude which is found in physics and chemistry. In fact, many natural sciences which deal with living phenomena such as botany and medicine are also not exact. Management is a social science like economics or psychology, and has the same limitations which these and other social sciences have. But this does not in any way diminish the value of management as a knowledge and discipline. It has provided powerful tools of analysis, prediction and control to practicing managers and helped them in performing their material tasks more efficiently and effectively.

Management as an art : Just as an engineer uses the science of engineering while building a bridge, a manager uses the knowledge of management theory while performing his managerial functions. Engineering is a science; its application to the solution of practical problems is an art. Similarly, management as a body of knowledge and a discipline is a science; its application to the solution of organizational problems is an art. The practice of management, like the practice of medicine, is firmly grounded in an identifiable body of concepts, theories and principles. A medical practitioner, who does not base his diagnosis and prescription on the science of medicine, endangers the life of his patient. Similarly, a manager who manages without possessing the knowledge of management creates chaos and jeopardizes the well-being of his organization.

Principles of management like the principles of medicine are used by the practitioner not as rules of thumb but as guides in solving practical problems. It is often said that managerial decision making involves a large element of judgement. This is true too. The raging controversy whether management is a science or an art is fruitless. It is a science as well as an art. Developments in the field of the knowledge of management help in the improvement of its practice; and improvements in the practice of management spur further research and study resulting in further development of management science.

Management as a Profession : We often hear of professionalisation of management in our country. By a professional manager, we generally mean a manager who undertakes management as a career and is not interested in acquiring ownership share in the enterprise which he manages. But, is management a profession in the true sense of the word? or, is management a profession like the professions of law and medicine? According to McFarland a profession possess the following characteristics : (i) a body of principles, techniques, skills, and specialized knowledge; (ii) formalized methods of acquiring training and experience; (iii) the establishment of a representative organization with professionalisation as its goal; (iv) the formation of ethical codes for the guidance of conduct; and (v) the charging of fees based on the nature of services.

Management is a profession to the extent it fulfils the above conditions. It is a profession in the sense that there is a systematized body of management, and it is distinct, identifiable discipline. It has also developed a vast number of tools and techniques. But unlike medicine or law, a management degree is not a prerequisite to become a manager. In fact, most managers in India as elsewhere do not have a formal management education. It seems reasonable to assume that at no time in the near future, the possession of a management degree will be a requirement for employment as a career manager.

Management is also a profession in the sense that formalized methods of training is available to those who desire to be managers. We have a number of institutes of management and university departments of management which provide formal education in this field. Training facilities are provided in most companies by their training divisions. A number of organizations such as the Administrative Staff College of India, the Indian Institutes of Management, Management Development Institute, the All India Management Association, and the university departments of management offer a variety of short-term management training programmes.

Management partially fulfils the third characteristic of profession. There are a number of representative organizations of management practitioners almost in all countries such as the All India Management Association in

India, the American Management Association in U.S.A., etc. However, none of them have professionalisation of management as its goal.

Management does not fulfill the last two requirements of a profession. There is no ethical code of conduct for managers as for doctors and lawyers. Some individual business organizations, however, try to develop a code of conduct for their own managers but there is no general and uniform code of conduct for all managers. In fact, bribing public officials to gain favours, sabotaging trade unions, manipulating prices and markets are by no means uncommon management practices. Furthermore, managers in general do not seem to adhere to the principle of "service above self". However little regard is paid to the elevation of service over the desire for monetary compensation is evidenced by switching of jobs by managers. Indeed, such mobile managers are regarded as more progressive and modern than others.

It may be concluded from the above discussion that management is a science, an art as well as a profession. As a social science, management is not as exact as natural sciences, and it is not as fully a profession as medicine and law.

1.6 MANAGEMENT VS. ADMINISTRATION

The use of two terms management and administration has been a controversial issue in the management literature. Some writers do not see any difference between the two terms, while others maintain that administration and management are two different functions. Those who held management and administration distinct include Oliver Sheldon, Florence and Tead, Spriegel and Lansburg, etc. According to them, management is a lower-level function and is concerned primarily with the execution of policies laid down by administration. But some English authors like Brech are of the opinion that management is a wider term including administration. This controversy is discussed as under in three heads:

(i) Administration is concerned with the determination of policies and management with the implementation of policies. Thus, administration is a higher level function.

(ii) Management is a generic term and includes administration.

(iii) There is no distinction between the terms management and administration and they are used interchangeably.

(i) **Administration is a Higher Level Function :** Oliver Shelden subscribed to the first viewpoint. According to him, "Administration is concerned with the determination of corporate policy, the coordination of finance, production and distribution, the settlement of the compass of the organization and the ultimate control of the executive. Management proper is concerned with the execution of policy within the limits set up by administration and the employment of the organization in the particular objects before it... Administration determines the organization; management uses it. Administration defines the goals; management strives towards it".

Administration refers to policy-making whereas management refers to execution of policies laid down by administration. This view is held by Tead, Spriegel and Walter. Administration is the phase of business enterprise that concerns itself with the overall determination of institutional objectives and the policies unnecessary to be followed in achieving those objectives. Administration is a determinative function; on the other hand, management is an executive function which is primarily concerned with carrying out of the broad policies laid down by the administration. Thus, administration involves broad policy-making and management involves the execution of policies laid down by the administration as shown in Table 1.

Table 1: Administration Vs. Management

	Basis	Administration	Management
1.	Meaning	Administration is concerned with the formulation of objectives, plans and policies of the organization	Management means getting the work done through and with others.
2.	Nature of work	Administration relates to the decision-making. It is a thinking function.	Management refers to execution of decisions. It is a doing function.
3.	Decision Making	Administration determines what is to be done and when it is to be done	Management decides who shall implement the administrative decisions.
4.	Status	Administration refers to higher levels of management	Management is relevant at lower levels in the organization.

(ii) **Management is a Generic Term :** The second viewpoint regards management as a generic term including administration. According to Brech, "Management is a social process entailing responsibility for the effective and economical planning and regulation of the operation of an enterprise in fulfillment of a given purpose or task. Administration is that part of management which is concerned with the installation and carrying out of the procedures by which the programme is laid down and communicated and the progress of activities is regulated and checked against plans". Thus, Brech conceives administration as a part of management. Kimball and Kimball also subscribe to this view. According to them administration is a part of management. Administration is concerned with the actual work of executing or carrying out the objectives.

(iii) **Management and Administration are Synonymous:** The third viewpoint is that there is no distinction between the terms 'management' and 'administration'. Usage also provides no distinction between these terms. The term management is used for higher executive functions like determination of policies, planning, organizing, directing and controlling in the business circles, while the term administration is used for the same set of functions in the Government circles. So there is no difference between these two terms and they are often used interchangeably.

It seems from the above concepts of administration and management that administration is the process of determination of objectives, laying down plans and policies, and ensuring that achievements are in conformity with the objectives. Management is the process of executing the plans and policies for the achievement of the objectives determined by an administration. This distinction seems to be too simplistic and superficial. If we regard chairmen, managing directors and general managers as performing administrative functions, it cannot be said that they perform only planning functions of goal determination, planning and policy formulation, and do not perform other functions such as staffing functions of selection and promotion, or directing functions of leadership, communication and motivation. On the other hand, we cannot say that managers who are responsible for the execution of plans and formulation of plans and policies, etc. do not contribute to the administrative functions of goal determination, and formulation of plans and policies. In fact all manages, whether the chief executive or the first line supervisor, are in some way or the other involved in the performance of all the managerial functions. It is, of course, true that those who occupy the higher echelons of organizational hierarchy are involved to a greater extent in goal determination, plans and policy formulation and organizing than those who are at the bottom of the ladder.

1.7 LEVELS OF MANAGEMENT

An enterprise may have different levels of management. Levels of management refer to a line of demarcation between various managerial positions in an enterprise. The levels of management depend upon its size, technical facilities, and the range of production. We generally come across two broad levels of management, viz. (i) administrative management (i.e., the upper level of management) and (ii) operating management (i.e., the lower level of management). Administrative management is concerned with "thinking" functions such as laying down policy, planning and setting up of standards. Operative management is concerned with the "doing" function such as implementation of policies, and directing the operations to attain the objectives of the enterprise.

But in actual practice, it is difficult to draw any clear cut demarcation between thinking function and doing function. Because the basic/fundamental managerial functions are performed by all managers irrespective of their levels or, ranks. For instance, wage and salary director of a company may assist in fixing wages and salary structure as a member of the Board of Directors, but as head of wages and salary department, his job is to see that the decisions are implemented.

The real significance of levels is that they explain authority relationships in an organization. Considering the hierarchy of authority and responsibility, one can identify three levels of management namely:

(i) **Top management** of a company consists of owners/shareholders, Board of Directors, its Chairman, Managing Director, or the Chief Executive, or the General Manager or Executive Committee having key officers.

(ii) Middle management of a company consists of heads of functional departments viz. Purchase Manager, Production Manager, Marketing Manager, Financial controller, etc. and Divisional and Sectional Officers working under these Functional Heads.

(iii) Lower level or operative management of a company consists of Superintendents, Foremen, Supervisors, etc.

1. **Top management :** Top management is the ultimate source of authority and it lays down goals, policies and plans for the enterprise. It devotes more time on planning and coordinating functions. It is accountable to the owners of the business of the overall management. It is also described as the policy making group responsible for the overall direction and success of all company activities. The important functions of top management include :

    (a) To establish the objectives or goals of the enterprise.

    (b) To make policies and frame plans to attain the objectives laid.

    (c) To set up an organizational frame work to conduct the operations as per plans.

    (d) To assemble the resources of money, men, materials, machines and methods to put the plans into action.

    (e) To exercise effective control of the operations.

    (f) To provide overall leadership to the enterprise.

2. **Middle management :** The job of middle management is to implement the policies and plans framed by the top management. It serves as an essential link between the top management and the lower level or operative management. They are responsible to the top management for the functioning of their departments. They devote more time on the organization and motivation functions of management. They provide the guidance and the structure for a purposeful enterprise. Without them the top

management's plans and ambitious expectations will not be fruitfully realized. The following are the main functions of middle management:

(a) To interpret the policies chalked out by top management.

(b) To prepare the organizational set up in their own departments for fulfilling the objectives implied in various business policies.

(c) To recruit and select suitable operative and supervisory staff.

(d) To assign activities, duties and responsibilities for timely implementation of the plans.

(e) To compile all the instructions and issue them to supervisor under their control.

(f) To motivate personnel to attain higher productivity and to reward them properly.

(g) To cooperate with the other departments for ensuring a smooth functioning of the entire organization.

(h) To collect reports and information on performance in their departments.

(i) To report to top management

(j) To make suitable recommendations to the top management for the better execution of plans and policies.

3. **Lower or operative management:** It is placed at the bottom of the hierarchy of management, and actual operations are the responsibility of this level of management. It consists of foreman, supervisors, sales officers, accounts officers and so on. They are in direct touch with the rank and file or workers. Their authority and responsibility is limited. They pass on the instructions of the middle management to workers.

They interpret and divide the plans of the management into short-range operating plans. They are also involved in the process of decisions-making. They have to get the work done through the workers. They allot various jobs to the workers, evaluate their performance and report to the middle level management. They are more concerned with direction and control functions of management. They devote more time in the supervision of the workers.

1.8 MANAGERIAL SKILLS

A skill is an individual's ability to translate knowledge into action. Hence, it is manifested in an individual's performance. Skill is not necessarily inborn. It can be developed through practice and through relating learning to one's own personal experience and background. In order to be able to successfully discharge his roles, a manager should possess three major skills. These are conceptual skill, human relations skill and technical skill. Conceptual skill deals with ideas, technical skill with things and human skill with people. While both conceptual and technical skills are needed for good decision-making, human skill in necessary for a good leader.

The *conceptual skill* refers to the ability of a manager to take a broad and farsighted view of the organization and its future, his ability to think in abstract, his ability to analyze the forces working in a situation, his creative and innovative ability and his ability to assess the environment and the changes taking place in it. It short, it is his ability to conceptualize the environment, the organization, and his own job, so that he can set appropriate goals for his organization, for himself and for his team. This skill seems to increase in importance as manager moves up to higher positions of responsibility in the organization.

The *technical skill* is the manager's understanding of the nature of job that people under him have to perform. It refers to a person's knowledge and proficiency in any type of process or technique. In a production department this would mean an understanding of the technicalities of the process of production. Whereas this type of skill and competence seems to be more important at the lower levels of management, its relative importance as a part of the managerial role diminishes as the manager moves to higher positions. In higher functional positions, such as the position of a marketing manager or production manager, the conceptual component, related to these functional areas becomes more important and the technical component becomes less important.

Human relations skill is the ability to interact effectively with people at all levels. This skill develops in the manager sufficient ability (a) to recognize the feelings and sentiments of others; (b) to judge the possible actions to, and outcomes of various courses of action he may undertake; and (c) to examine his own concepts and values which may enable him to develop more useful attitudes about himself. This type of skill remains consistently important for managers at all levels.

Table-2 gives an idea about the required change in the skill-mix of a manager with the change in his level. At the top level, technical skill becomes least important. That is why, people at the top shift with great ease from one industry to another without an apparent fall in their efficiency. Their human and conceptual skills seem to make up for their unfamiliarity with the new job's technical aspects.

Tables-2 : Skill-mix of different management levels

Top Management ⟶ Conceptual Skills

Middle Management ⟶ Human Relations Skills

Low Management ⟶ Technical Skills

1.9 THE MANAGER AND HIS JOB

Management performs the functions of planning, organizing, staffing, directing and controlling for the accomplishment of organizational goals. Any person who performs these functions is a manager. The first line manager or supervisor or foreman is also a manager because he performs these functions. The difference between the functions of top, middle and lowest level management is that of degree. For instance, top management concentrates more on long-range planning and organization, middle level management concentrates more on coordination and control and lowest level management concentrates more on direction function to get the things done from the workers.

Every manager is concerned with ideas, things and people. Management is a creative process for integrating the use of resources to accomplish certain goals. In this process, ideas, things and people are vital inputs which are to be transformed into output consistent with the goals.

Management of ideas implies use of conceptual skills. It has three connotations. *First*, it refers to the need for practical philosophy of management to regard management as a distinct and scientific process. *Second*, management of ideas refers to the planning phase of management process. *Lastly*, management of ideas refers to distinction and innovation. Creativity refers to generation of new ideas, and innovation refers to transforming ideas into viable relations and utilities. A manager must be imaginative to plan ahead and to create new Ideas.

Management of things (non-human resources) deal with the design of production system, and acquisition, allocation and conversion of physical resources to achieve certain goals. Management of people is concerned with procurement, development, maintenance and integration of human resources in the organization. Every manager has to direct his subordinates to put the organizational plans into practice.

The greater part of every manager's time is spent in communicating and dealing with people. His efforts are directed towards obtaining information and evaluating progress towards objectives set by him and then taking corrective action. Thus, a manager's job primarily consists of management of people. Though it is his duty to handle all the productive resources, but human factor is more important. A manager cannot convert the raw materials into finished products himself; he has to take the help of others to do this. The greatest problem before any manager is how to manage the personnel to get the best possible results. The manager in the present age has to deal efficiently with the people who are to contribute for the achievement of organizational goals.

Peter F. Drucker has advocated that the managerial approach to handle workers and work should be pragmatic and dynamic. Every job should be designed as an integrated set of operations. The workers should be given a sufficient measure of freedom to organize and control their work environment. It is the duty of every manager to educate, train and develop people below him so that they may use their potentialities and abilities to perform the work allotted to them. He has also to help them in satisfying their needs and working under him, he must provide them with proper environment. A manager must create a climate which brings in and maintains satisfaction and discipline among the people. This will increase organizational effectiveness.

Recently, it has been questioned whether planning, organizing, directing and controlling provides an adequate description of the management process. After an intensive observation of what five top executive actually did during the course of a few days at work, Henry Mintzberg concluded that these labels do not adequately capture the reality of what managers do. He suggested instead that the manager should be regarded as playing some ten different roles, in no particular order.

Role Performed by Managers

1. **Interpersonal Roles**

    Figurehead : In this role, every manager has to perform some duties of a ceremonial nature, such as greeting the touring dignitaries, attending the wedding of an employee, taking an important customer to lunch and so on.

    Leader : As a leader, every manager must motivate and encourage his employees. He must also try to reconcile their individual needs with the goals of the organization.

    Liaison : In this role of liaison, every manager must cultivate contacts outside his vertical chain of command to collect information useful for his organization.

2. **Informational Roles**

    Monitor : As monitor, the manager has to perpetually scan his environment for information, interrogate his liaison contacts and his subordinates, and receive unsolicited information, much of it as result of the network of personal contacts he has developed.

    Disseminator: In the role of a disseminator, the manager passes some of his privileged information directly to his subordinates who would otherwise have no access to it.

Spokesman : In this role, the manager informs and satisfies various groups and people who influence his organization. Thus, he advises shareholders about financial performance, assures consumer groups that the organization is fulfilling its social responsibilities and satisfies government that the origination is abiding by the law.

3. **Decisional Roles**

   Entrepreneur : In this role, the manager constantly looks out for new ideas and seeks to improve his unit by adapting it to changing conditions in the environment.

   Disturbance Handler : In this role, the manager has to work like a fire fighter. He must seek solutions of various unanticipated problems – a strike may loom large a major customer may go bankrupt; a supplier may renege on his contract, and so on.

   Resource Allocator : In this role, the manager must divide work and delegate authority among his subordinates. He must decide who will get what.

   Negotiator : The manager has to spend considerable time in negotiations. Thus, the chairman of a company may negotiate with the union leaders a new strike issue, the foreman may negotiate with the workers a grievance problem, and so on.

   In addition, managers in any organization work with each other to establish the organization's long-range goals and to plan how to achieve them. They also work together to provide one another with the accurate information needed to perform tasks. Thus, managers act as channels of communication with the organization.

Characteristics of Professional Managers

1. **Managers are responsible and accountable :** Managers are responsible for seeing that specific tasks are done successfully. They are usually evaluated on how well they arrange for these tasks to the accomplished. Managers are responsible for the actions of their subordinates. The success or failure of subordinates is a direct reflection of managers' success or failure. All members of an organization, including those who are not managers, are responsible for their particular tasks. The difference is that managers are held responsible, or accountable, not only for their own work, but also for the work of subordinates.

2. **Managers balance competing goals and set priorities :** At any given time, the manager faces a number of organizational goals, problems and needs all of which compete for the manager's time and resources (both human and material). Because such resources are always limited, the manager must strike a balance between the various goals and needs. Many managers, for example, arrange each day's tasks in order of priority the most important things are done right away, while the less important tasks are looked at later. In this way, managerial time is used effectively.

   A manager must also decide who is to perform a particular task and must assign work to an appropriate person. Although ideally each person should be given the task he would most like to do, this is not always possible. Sometimes individual ability is the decisive factor, and a task is assigned to the person most able to accomplish it. But sometimes a less capable worker is assigned a task as a learning experience. And, at times, limited human or other resources dictate decisions for making work assignments. Managers are often caught between conflicting human and organizational needs and so they must identify priorities.

3. **Managers think analytically and conceptually :** To be an analytical thinker, a manager must be able to break a problem down into its components, analyze those components and then come up with a feasible solution. But even more important, a manager must be a conceptual thinker, able to view the entire task in the abstract and relate it to other tasks. Thinking about a particular task in relation to its larger implications is no simple matter. But it is essential if the manager is to work towards the goals of the organization as a whole as well as towards the goals of an individual unit.

4. **Managers are mediators :** Organizations are made up of people, and people disagree or quarrel quite often. Disputes within a unit or organization can lower morale and productivity, and they may become so unpleasant or disruptive that competent employees decide to leave the organization. Such occurrences hinder work towards the goals of the unit or organization; therefore, managers must at times take on the role of mediator and iron out disputes before they get out of hand. Setting conflicts requires skill and tact. Managers who are careless in their handling conflicts may later on find that they have only made matters worse.

5. **Managers make difficult decisions :** No organization runs smoothly all the time. There is almost no limit to the number and types of problems that may occur : financial difficulties, problems with employees, or differences of opinion concerning an organization policy, to name just a few. Managers are expected to come up with solutions to difficult problems and to follow through on their decisions even when doing so may be unpopular.

This description of these managerial roles and responsibilities shows that managers must 'change hats' frequently and must be alert to the particular role needed at a given time. The ability to recognize the appropriate role to be played and to change roles readily is a mark of an effective manager.

1.10 PRINCIPLES OF MANAGEMENT

A body of principles of management has been developed by Henri Fayol, the father of modern management. Fayol wrote perceptibly on the basis of his practical experience as a manager. Although, he did not develop an integrated theory of management, his principles are surprisingly in tune with contemporary thinking in management theory.

Fayol held that there is a single "administrative science", whose principles can be used in all management situations no matter what kind of organization was being managed. This earned him the title of "Universality". He, however, emphasized that his principles were not immutable laws but rules of thumb to be used as occasion demanded.

Fayol held that activities of an industrial enterprise can be grouped in six categories : (i) technical (production), (ii) commercial (buying, selling and exchange), (iii) financial (search for and optimum use of capital), (iv) security (protection of property and persons), (v) accounting (including statistics); and (vi) managerial. However, he devoted most of his attention to managerial activity. He developed the following principles underlying management of all kinds of organizations :

1. **Authority and Responsibility are Related :** Fayol held that authority flows from responsibility. Managers who exercise authority over others should assume responsibility for decisions as well as for results. He regarded authority as a corollary to responsibility. Authority is official as well as personal. Official

authority is derived from the manager's position in organizational hierarchy and personal authority is compounded of intelligence, experience, moral worth, past services, etc.

A corollary of the principle that no manager should be given authority unless he assumes responsibility is that those who have responsibility should also have commensurate authority in order to enable them to initiate action on others and command resources required for the performance of their functions. This aspect of relationship between responsibility and authority is particularly relevant in India where authority tends to be concentrated in higher echelons of management.

2. **Unity of Command :** This principle holds that one employee should have only one boss and receive instructions from him only. Fayol observed that if this principle is violated authority will be undermined, discipline will be jeopardy, order will be disturbed and stability will be threatened. Dual command is a permanent source of conflict. Therefore, in every organization, each subordinate should have one superior whose command he has to obey.

3. **Unity of Direction :** This means that all managerial and operational activities which relate a distinct group with the same objective should be directed by "one head and one plan. According to Fayol, there should be, "one head and one plan for a group of activities having the same objective". It, however, does not mean that all decisions should be made at the top. It only means that all related activities should be directed by one person. For example, all marketing activities like product strategy and policy, advertising and sales promotion, distribution channel policy, product pricing policy, marketing research, etc., should be under the control of one manager

38

and directed by an integrated plan. This is essential for the "unity of action, coordination of strength and focusing of effort". Violation of this principle will cause fragmentation of action and effort, and wastage of resources.

4. **Scalar Chain of Command :** According to Fayol scalar chain is the chain of superiors ranging from the ultimate authority to the lowest ranks. The line of authority is the route followed via every link in the chain by all communication which start from or go to the ultimate authority.

5. **Division of Work :** This is the principle of specialization which, according to Fayol, applies to all kinds of work, managerial as well as technical. It helps a person to acquire an ability and accuracy with which he can do more and better work with the same effort. Therefore, the work of every person in the organization should be limited as far as possible to the performance of a single leading function.

6. **Discipline :** Discipline is a *sine qua non* for the proper functioning of an organization. Members of an organization are required to perform their functions and conduct themselves in relation to others according to rules, norms and customs. According to Fayol, discipline can best be maintained by : (i) having good superiors at all levels; (ii) agreements (made either with the individual employees or with a union as the case may be) that are as clear and fair as possible; and (iii) penalties judiciously imposed.

7. **Subordination of Individual Interest to General Interest :** The interest of the organization is above the interests of the individual and the group. It can be achieved only when managers in high positions in the organization set an example of honesty, integrity, fairness and justice. It will involve an attitude and a spirit of sacrificing their own personal interests whenever it becomes apparent that such personal interests are in conflict with organizational interests. It may, however, be emphasized that social and national interests should have precedence over organizational interests whenever the two run counter to each other.

8. **Remuneration :** Employees should be paid fairly and equitably. Differentials in remuneration should be based on job differentials, in terms of qualities of the employee, application, responsibility, working conditions and difficulty of the job. It should also take into account factors like cost of living, general economic conditions, demand for labour and economic state of the business.

9. **Centralisation :** Fayol believed in centralisation. He, however, did not contemplate concentration of all decision making authority in the top management. He, however, held that centralisation and decentralisation is a question of proportion. In a small firm with a limited number of employees, the owner-manager can give orders directly to everyone. In large organizations, however, where the worker is separated from the chief executive through a long scalar chain, the decision making authority has to be distributed among various managers in varying degrees. Here one generally comes across a situation of decentralisation with centralised control. The degree of centralisation and decentralisation also depends on the quality of managers.

10. **Order :** Order, in the conception of Fayol, means right person on the right job and everything in its proper place. This kind of order, depends on precise knowledge of human requirements and resources of the concern and a constant balance between these requirements and resources.

11. **Equity :** It means that subordinates should be treated with justice and kindliness. This is essential for eliciting their devotion and loyalty to the enterprise. It is, therefore the duty of the chief executive to instill a sense of equity throughout all levels of scalar chain.

12. **Stability of Tenure of Personnel :** The managerial policies should provide a sense of reasonable job security. The hiring and firing of personnel should depend not on the whims of the superiors but on the well-conceived personnel policies. He points out that it takes time for an employee to learn his job; if they quit or are discharged within a short time, the learning time has been wasted. At the same time those found unsuitable should be removed and those who are found to be competent should be promoted. However, "a mediorce manager who stays is infinitely preferable to outstanding managers who come and go".

13. **Initiative :** It focuses on the ability, attitude and resourcefulness to act without prompting from others. Managers must create an environment which encourages their subordinates to take initiative and responsibility. Since it provides a sense of great satisfaction to intelligent employees, managers should sacrifice their personal vanity in order to encourage their subordinates to show initiative. It should, however, be limited, according to Fayol, by respect for authority and discipline.

14. **Esprit de Corps :** Cohesiveness and team spirit should be encouraged among employees. It is one of the chief characteristics of organized activity that a number of people work together in close coopearation for the achievement of common goals. An environment should be created in the organization which will induce people to contribute to each other's efforts in such a way that the combined effort of all together promotes the achievement of the overall objectives of enterprise. Fayol warns against two enemies of *esprit de corps*, viz. (i) divide and rule, and (ii) abuse of written communication. It may work to the benefit of the enterprise to divide its enemy but it will surely be dangerous to divide one's own workers. They should rather be welded in cohesive and highly interacting work-groups. Overreliance on written communication also tends to disrupt team spirit. Written communication, where necessary, should always be supplemented by oral communication because face-to-face contacts tend to promote speed, clarity and harmony.

The other important principles of management as developed by pioneer thinkers on the subject are :

(a) Separation of planning and execution of business operations.

(b) Scientific approach to business problems.

(c) Adoption of technological changes.

(d) Economizing production costs and avoiding the wastage of resources.

(e) Fuller utilization of the operational capacity and emphasis on higher productivity.

(f) Standardisation of tools, machines, materials, methods, timings and products.

(g) Evaluation of results according to criteria of standard levels of performance.

(h) Understanding and co-operation among the members of the organization set-up.

1.11 SIGNIFICANCE OF MANAGEMENT

Management is concerned with acquiring maximum prosperity with a minimum effort. Management is essential wherever group efforts are required to be directed towards achievement of common goals. In this management conscious age, the significance of management can hardly be over emphasized. It is said that, anything minus management amounts to nothing. Koontz and O' Donnel have rightly observed "there is no more important area of human activity than management since its task is that of getting things done through others."

The significance of management in business activities is relatively greater. The inputs of labour, capital and raw material never become productive without the catalyst of management. It is now widely recognized that management is an important factor of growth of any country. The following points further highlight the significance of management :

1. **Achievements of group goals :** Management makes group efforts more effective. The group as a whole cannot realise its objectives unless and until there is mutual co-operation and co-ordination among the members of the group. Management creates team work and team spirit in an organization by developing a sound organization structure. It brings the human and material resources

together and motivates the people for the achievement of the goals of the organization.

2. **Optimum utilization of resources :** Management always concentrates on achieving the objectives of the enterprise. The available resources of production are put to use in such a way that all sort of wastage and inefficiencies are reduced to a minimum. Workers are motivated to put in their best performance by the inspiring leadership. Managers create and maintain an environment conducive to highest efficiency and performance. Through the optimum use of available resources, management accelerates the process of economic growth.

3. **Minimisation of cost :** In the modern era of intense competition, every business enterprise must minimise the cost of production and distribution. Only those concerns can survive in the market, which can produce goods of better quality at the minimum cost. A study of the principles of management helps in knowing certain techniques used for reducing costs. These techniques are production control, budgetary control, cost control, financial control, material control, etc.

4. **Change and growth :** A business enterprise operates in a constantly changing environment. Changes in business environment create uncertainties and risk and also produce opportunities for growth. An enterprise has to change and adjust itself in the everchanging environment. Sound management moulds not only the enterprise but also alters the environment itself to ensure the success of the business. Many of the giant business corporations of today had a

humble beginning and grew continuously through effective management.

5. **Efficient and smooth running of business :** Management ensures efficient and smooth running of business, through better planning, sound organization and effective control of the various factors of production.

6. **Higher profits :** Profits can be enhanced in any enterprise either by increasing the sales revenue or reducing costs. To increase the sales revenue is beyond the control of an enterprise. Management by decreasing costs increases its profits and thus provides opportunities for future growth and development.

7. **Provide innovation :** Management gives new ideas, imagination and visions to an enterprise.

8. **Social benefits :** Management is useful not only to the business firms but to the society as a whole. It improves the standard of living of the people through higher production and more efficient use of scarce resources. By establishing cordial relations between different social groups, management promotes peace and prosperity in society.

9. **Useful for developing countries :** Management has to play a more important role in developing countries, like India. In such countries, the productivity is low and the resources are limited. It has been rightly observed, "There are no under-developed countries. They are only under-managed ones".

10. **Sound organization structure :** Management establishes proper organization structure and avoids conflict between the superiors and subordinates. This helps in the development of spirit of cooperation and mutual understanding, and a congenial environment is provided in the organization.

1.12 SUMMARY

Management is the force that unifies various resources and is the process of bringing them together and coordinating them to help accomplish organization goal. Management is both, a science as well as art. It is an inexact science. However, its principles as distinguished from practice are of universal application. Management does not yet completely fulfill all the criteria of a profession. There are three levels of management - top, middle and lower. Managers at different levels of the organization require and use different types of skills. Lower level managers require and use a greater degree of technical skill than high level managers, while higher level managers require and use a greater degree of conceptual skill. Human skills are important at all managerial levels.

1.13 SELF ASSESSMENT QUESTIONS

1. "There is no important area of human activity than management since its task is that of getting things done through people". Discuss.

2. "Management is both a science and an art". Discuss this statement, giving suitable examples.

3. Define Management. How does it differ from Administration?

4. What do you understand by the term "Levels of Management"? Explain with reference to an organization with which you are familiar.

5. Briefly discuss the nature and scope of Management.

6. What are the functions of a Manager? Is mere knowledge of Management enough to become successful manager?

7. Discuss basic principles of Management along with their significance.

8. Discuss and illustrate the meaning, definition and characteristics of management in modern organizations.

9. What is Management? Explain the principles of management with suitable illustrations.

1.14 FURTHER READINGS

1. Kootnz & O'Donnell, Principles of Management.

2. J.S. Chandan, Management Concepts and Strategies.

3. Arun Kumar and R. Sharma, Principles of Business Management.

4. Sherlerkar and Sherlerkar, Principles of Management

5. B.P. Singh, Business Management and Organizations

EVOLUTION OF MANAGEMENT THOUGHTS

Objective: The objective of this lesson is to discuss and make out various management thoughts and approaches and their applicability in present context.

Lesson Structure

2.1 Introduction to Management Thoughts

2.2 Forces Backing Management Thoughts

2.3 A Framework for the Management Thoughts

2.4 Major Contributions of Leading Management Thinkers

2.5 Approaches to the Study of Management

2.6 Summary

2.7 Self Assessment Exercise

2.8 Suggested Readings

2.1 INTRODUCTION

Organized endeavors, directed by people, responsible for planning, organizing, leading and controlling activities have been in existence for thousands of years. Management has been practiced in some form or the other since the dawn of civilization. Ever since human beings started living together in groups, techniques of organization and management were evolved. The Egyptian pyramids, the Chinese Civil Service, The Roman Catholic Church, the military organizations and the Great Wall of China, for instance, are tangible evidence that projects of tremendous scope, employing tens of thousands of people, were undertaken well before the modern times.

The pyramids are particularly interesting examples. The construction of a single pyramid occupied more than 1,00,000 workers for 20 years. Who told each worker that what did one do? Who ensured that there would be enough stones at the site to keep the workers busy? The answer is Managers, regardless of what managers were called at that time. He had to plan what was to be done, organize people and material to do it, lead and direct the workers, and impose some controls to ensure that everything was done as planned. This example from the past demonstrates that organizations have been around for thousands of years and that management has been practices for an equivalent period. However, two pre-twentieth-century events played significant roles in promoting the study of management. First is Adam Smith's contribution in the field of management and second is influence of Industrial Revolution in management practice.

1) *Adam Smith's* name is typically cited in field of economics for his contribution to classical economic doctrine, but his contribution in Wealth of Nations (1776) outlined the economic advantage that organization and society can gain from the *division of labor*. He used the pin-manufacturing industry for his example. Smith noted that 10 individuals, each doing a specialized task, could produce about 4800 pins a day. However, if each worked separately and had to perform each task, it

would be quite an accomplishment to produce even 10 pins a day. Smith concluded that division of labor increased productivity by increasing each worker's skill and dexterity, by saving time lost in changing tasks, and by creating labor-saving inventions and machinery.

2) ***Industrial Revolution*** is another most important aspect that influences management in pre-twentieth century. The major contribution of the industrial revolution was the substitution of machine power for human power, which in turn, made it more economical to manufacture goods in factories. The advent of machine power, mass production, the reduced transportation costs that followed a rapid expansion of the railroads and lack of governmental regulation also fostered the development of big organization.

Now, a formal theory to guide managers in running their organization was needed. However, it was not until the early 1900s that the first major step toward developing such a theory was taken. The periods of evaluation of management thoughts are highlighted in the *Table-2.1*:

TABLE-2.1 EVOLUTION OF MANAGEMENT THOUGHTS

MANAGEMENT THOUGHTS	PERIOD
• Early Contributions	Upto 19th century
• Scientific Management	1900-1930
• Administrative/operational management	1916-1940
• Human relations approach	1930-1950
• Social systems approach	1940-1950
• Decision theory approach	1945-1965
• Management science approach	1950-1960
• Human behavior approach	1950-1970
• Systems approach	1960s onwards
• Contingency approach	1970s onwards

Thus, management has been recognized and identified as a distinctive branch of academic discipline in the twentieth century.

2.2 FORCES BACKING MANAGEMENT THOUGHTS

Management thoughts have took birth/evolved under the anxiety of political, social and economic forces. These are explained as follows:

1. ***Political Forces***: Management thoughts have been shaped by the political forces manifested through the administration of political institutions and government agencies. The important political forces includes the political assumptions with respect to property rights, contractual rights, concepts of justice, judicial processes and attitudes towards governmental control versus laissez-faire. Legal processes which emanate from political pressures, such as the Union Carbide disaster in Bhopal, have a tremendous impact on management thinking and practice. Political pressures also define the interrelated rights of consumers, suppliers, labour, owners, creditors and different segments of public.

2. ***Social Forces***: These evolve from the values and beliefs of a particular culture of people. The needs, education, religion and norms of human behaviour dictate the relations among people, which form social contracts. *Social contracts*, is that unwritten but understood set of rules that govern the behaviour of the people in their day-to-day interrelationships. The same happens between corporations and their constituents- labour, investors, creditors, suppliers and consumers. These social contracts defined relationships, responsibilities and liabilities that influence the development of management thoughts. It gives the society a sense of order and trust in which human affairs can be conducted in relative security and confidence.

3. ***Economic Forces***: These forces determine the scarcity, transformation and distribution of goods and services in a society. Every social institution competes for a limited amount of human, financial, physical and information resources. This competition over scarce resources allocates them to their most profitable use and is the motivator of technological innovation by which resource availability can be maximized.

2.3 A FRAMEWORK FOR THE MANAGEMENT THOUGHTS

In the past, the business houses, particularly corporates, did not have a high academic stature and position in the society and it certainly compelled the scholars inculcate the academic interest in the study of business management so that its real fruits could be realized for the stakeholders under reference. There was a widespread belief that management process consisted of hidden tricks, mysterious clues and intuitive knowledge that could be mastered only by a few divinely gifted people. Moreover, the businessmen were very much afraid that through the study of management their tricks and secrets would be exposed.

But the advent of industrial revolution and the introduction of large scale mechanized production and the resultant growth of trade, industry and commerce necessitated the study of management. The evolution of management thoughts might be better approached through the framework as depicted in *Figure-2.1*. In the beginning there were two classical schools of management thoughts. These were- the scientific management school and the organizational school. Later on, behavioural school and the quantitative school came into existence. These four schools merged into integration school which led to the contemporary school of management thoughts.

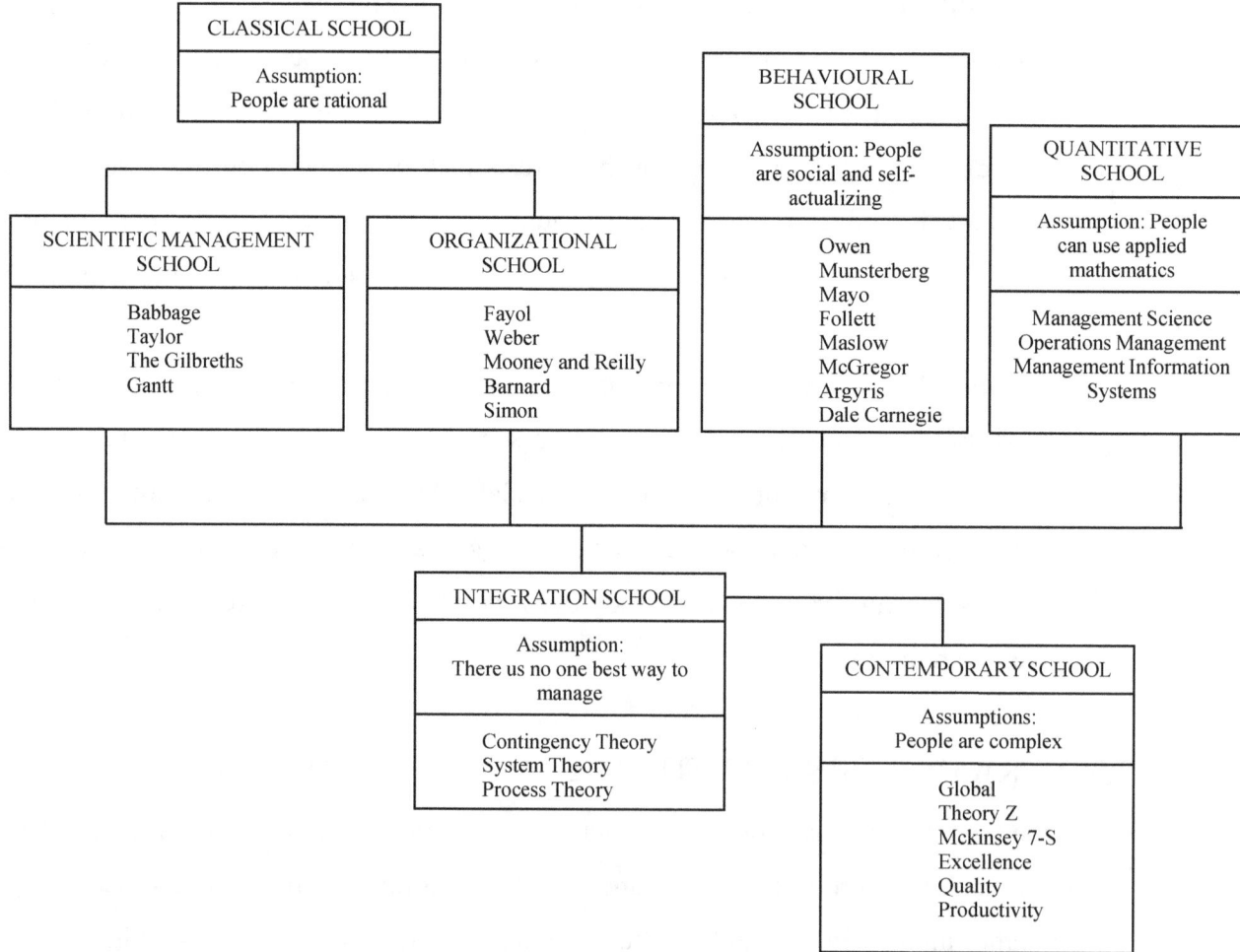

Figure- 2. 1   FRAMEWORK FOR THE MANAGEMENT THOUGHTS

Among the people who were in search of management principles, techniques and processes, a few emerged as outstanding pioneers. These are- Urwick and Brech, Boulton and Watt, Robert Owen, Charles Babbage, Oliver Sheldon, Lyndall Urwick, Herbert A. Simon, Frederick Winslow Taylor, H.S. Person, Henry L. Gantt, Frank Gilbreth, Harrington Emerson, H.P. Kendall, C.B. Barth, F.A. Halsey, Henri Dennison, Mooney and Reiley, Chester I. Barnard, Elton Mayo, F.J. Roethlisberger and T.N.Whitehead, Mary Parker Follett and Henry Fayol etc.

2.4 CONTRIBUTION OF LEADING THINKERS

1. **Classical School:** The classical development of management thoughts can be divided into- the scientific management, the organizational management, the behavioural management and the quantitative management. The first two (scientific management school and organizational) emerged in late 1800s and early 1900s were based on the management belief that people were rational, economic creatures choose a course of action that provide the greatest economic gain. These schools of management thoughts are explained as below:

(A) Scientific Management School: Scientific management means application of the scientific methods to the problem of management. It conducts a business or affairs by standards established by facts or truth gained through systematic observation, experiments, or reasoning. The followings individuals contribute in development of scientific management school of management thoughts. They dedicated to the increase in efficiency of labour by the management of the workers in the organization's technical core. They are:

   I. **Charles Babbage (1792-1871):** He was professor of mathematics at Cambridge University from 1828 to 1839. He concentrated on developing the efficiencies of labour production. He, like Adam Smith, was a proponent of the specialization of labour, and he applied mathematics to the efficient use of both production materials and facilities. He wrote nine books and over 70 papers on mathematics, science and philosophy. He advocated that the managers should conduct time studies data to establish work standards for anticipated work performance levels and to reward the workers with bonuses to the extent by which they exceed their standards. His best known book is 'On the Economy of Machinary and Manufacturers' published in 1832. He visited many factories in England and France and he found that manufacturers were totally unscientific and most of their work is guess work. He perceived that methods of science and mathematics could be applied to the operations of factories. His main contributions are as follows:

- He stressed the importance of division of and assignment to labour on the basis of skill.
- He recommended profit-sharing programs in an effort to foster harmonious management-labour relations.
- He stressed the means of determining the feasibility of replacing manual operations with machines.

II. **Fredrick W. Taylor (1856-1915):** He is known as 'father of scientific management'. His ideas about management grew out of his wide-ranging experience in three companies: Midvale Steel Works, Simonds Rolling Mills and Bethlehem Steel Co.

TABLE-2.2 TAYLOR'S FOUR PRINCIPLES OF SCIENTIFIC MANAGEMENT

Taylor's Principle	Related Management Activity
1. Develop a science for each job with standardized work implements and efficient methods for all to follow.	Complete time-and-motion study to determine the best way to do each task.
2. Scientifically select workers with skills and abilities that match each job, and train them in the most efficient ways to accomplish tasks.	Use job descriptions to select employees, set up formal training systems, and establish optimal work standards to follow.
3. Ensure cooperation through incentives and provide the work environment that reinforces optimal work results in a scientific manner.	Develop incentive pay, such as piece-rate system, to reward productivity, and encourage safe condition by using proper implements.
4. Divide responsibility for managing and for working, while supporting individuals in work groups for what they do best. Some people are more	Promote leaders who guide, not do, the work; create a sense of responsibility for group results by panning tasks and helping workers to achieve those results.

| capable of managing, whereas others are better at performing tasks laid out for them. | |

Source: Holt, 1990, p-38

As an engineer and consultant, Taylor observed and reported on what he found to be inexcusably inefficient work practices, especially in the steel industry. Taylor believed that workers output was only about one-third of what was possible. Therefore, he set out to correct the situation by applying scientific methods. Taylor's philosophy and ideas are given in his book, 'Principles of Scientific Management' published in 1911. Taylor gave the following principles of scientific management. These are outlined in Table- 2.2:

Taylor concluded that scientific management involves a completer mental revolution on the part of both workers and management, without this mental revolution scientific management does not exist.

III. **Henry Gantt (1861-1919):** He was a consulting engineer who specialized in control system for shop scheduling. He sought to increase workers efficiency through scientific investigation. He developed the *Gantt Chart* (Figure-2.2) that provides a graphic representation of the flow of the work required to complete a given task. The chart represents each planned stage of work, showing both scheduled times and actual times. Gantt Charts were used by managers as a scheduling device for planning and controlling work. Gantt devised an incentive system that gave workers a bonus for completing their job in less time than the allowed standards. His bonus systems were similar to the modern *gain sharing* techniques whereby employees are motivated to higher levels of performance by the potential of sharing in the profit generated. In doing so, Gantt expanded the scope of scientific management to encompass the work of managers as well as that of operatives.

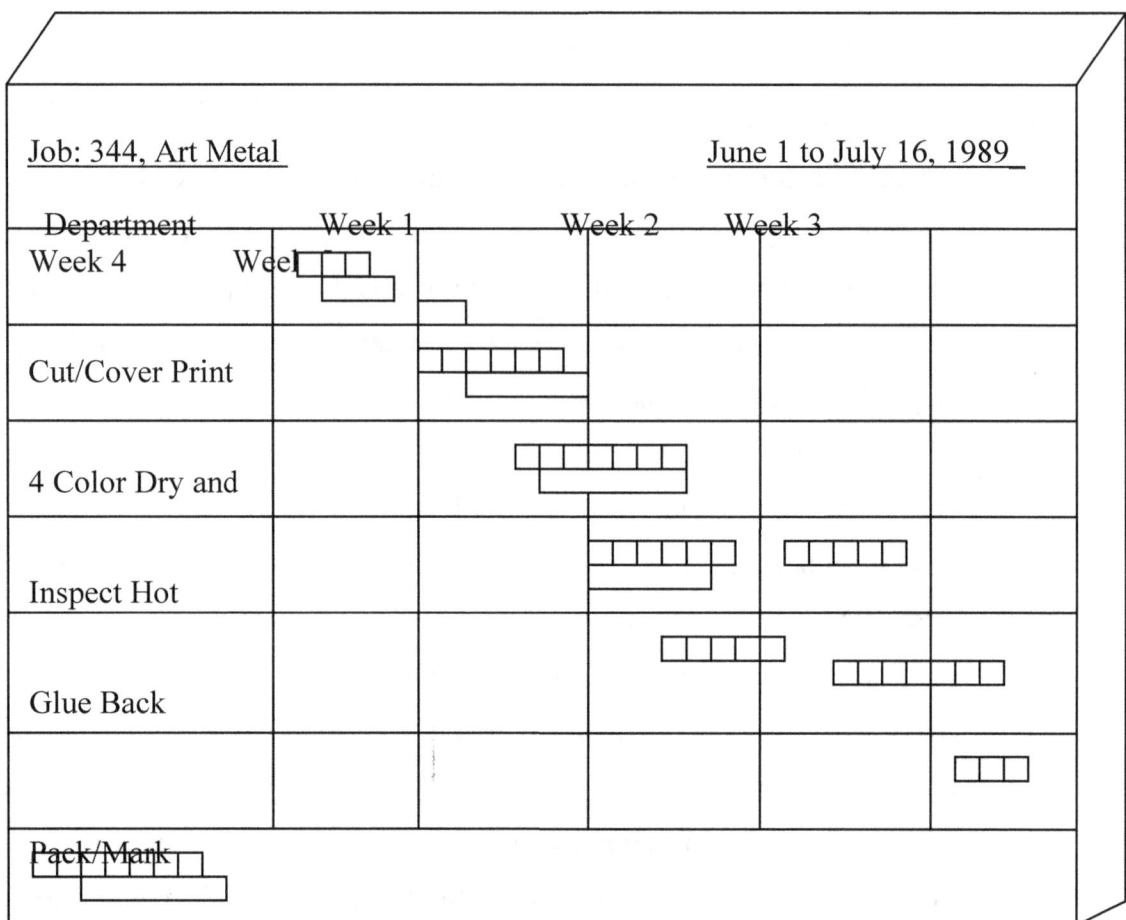

FIGURE-2.2 GANTT CHART FOR BOOK BINDERY

IV. **Frank (1868-1924) and Lillian (1878-1972) Gilbreth**: Frank Gilbreth, a construction contractor by back ground, gave up his contracting career in 1912 to study scientific management after hearing Taylor's speak at a professional meeting. Along with his wife Lillian, a psychologist, he studied work arrangements to eliminate wasteful hand-body-motion. Frank specialized in research that had a dramatic impact on medical surgery and, through his time and motion findings, surgeons saved many lives. Lillian is known as 'first lady of management' and devoted most of her research to the human side of management. Frank Gilbreth is probably best known for his experiments in reducing the number of motions in bricklaying.

The man and wife team developed a classification scheme for the various motions (17 basic hand motions) used to complete a job referring a motion as a *therblig*.

Their classification design covered such motions as grasping, moving, and holding. This scheme allowed him to more precisely analyze the exact elements of worker's hand movements. Their scientific motion scheme noted the relationship between types and frequencies of motions and the creation of workers fatigue, identifying that unnecessary or awkward motions were a waste of workers energy. By eliminating inappropriate motions and focusing on appropriate motion, the Gilbreth methodology reduces work fatigue and improves workers performance.

Gilbreth were among the first to use motion pictures films to study hand-and-body motions. They devised a micro chronometer that recorded time to 1/2,000 of a second, placed it in the field of the study being photographed and thus determined how long a worker spent enacting each motion. Wasted motions missed by the naked eyes could be identified and eliminated. Gilbreths also experimented with the design and use of the proper tools and equipments for optimizing work performance.

(B) **Organizational School:** The organizational school of management placed emphasis on the development of management principles for managing the complete organization. The contributors of organizational schools are:

I **Henri Fayol (1841-1925):** was a Frenchman with considerable executive experience who focused his research on the things that managers do. He wrote during the same period Taylor did. Taylor was a scientist and he was managing director of a large French coal-mining firm. He was the first to envisage a functional process approach to the practice of management. His was a functional approach because it defined the functions that must be performed by managers. It was also a process approach because he conceptualized the managerial job in a series of stages such as planning, organizing and controlling. According to Fayol, all managerial tasks could be classified into one of the following six groups:

- Technical (related to production);
- Commercial (buying, selling and exchange);
- Financial (search for capital and its optimum use);

- Security (protection for property and person);
- Accounting (recording and taking stock of costs, profits, and liabilities, keeping balance sheets, and compiling statistics);
- Managerial (planning, organizing, commanding, coordinating and control);

He pointed out that these activities exist in every organization. He focused his work on the administrative or managerial activities and developed the following definition:

- Planning meant developing a course of action that would help the organization achieve its objectives.
- Organizing meant mobilizing the employees and other resources of the organization in accordance with the plan.
- Commanding meant directing the employees and getting the job done.
- Coordinating meant achieving harmony among the various activities.
- Controlling meant monitoring performance to ensure that the plan is properly followed.

II *Max Weber (1864-1920):* He was a German sociologist. Writing in the early 1900s, Weber developed a theory of authority structures and described organizational activities on the basis of authority relations. He described an ideal type of organization that he called a bureaucracy, a form of organization characterized by division of labour, a clearly defined hierarchy, detailed rules and regulations, and impersonal relationships. Weber recognized that this ideal bureaucracy didn't exist in reality. He used it as a basis for theorizing about work and the way that work could be done in large groups. His theory became the model structural design for many of today's large organizations. The features of Weber's ideal bureaucratic structure are outlined in *Figure-2.3*:

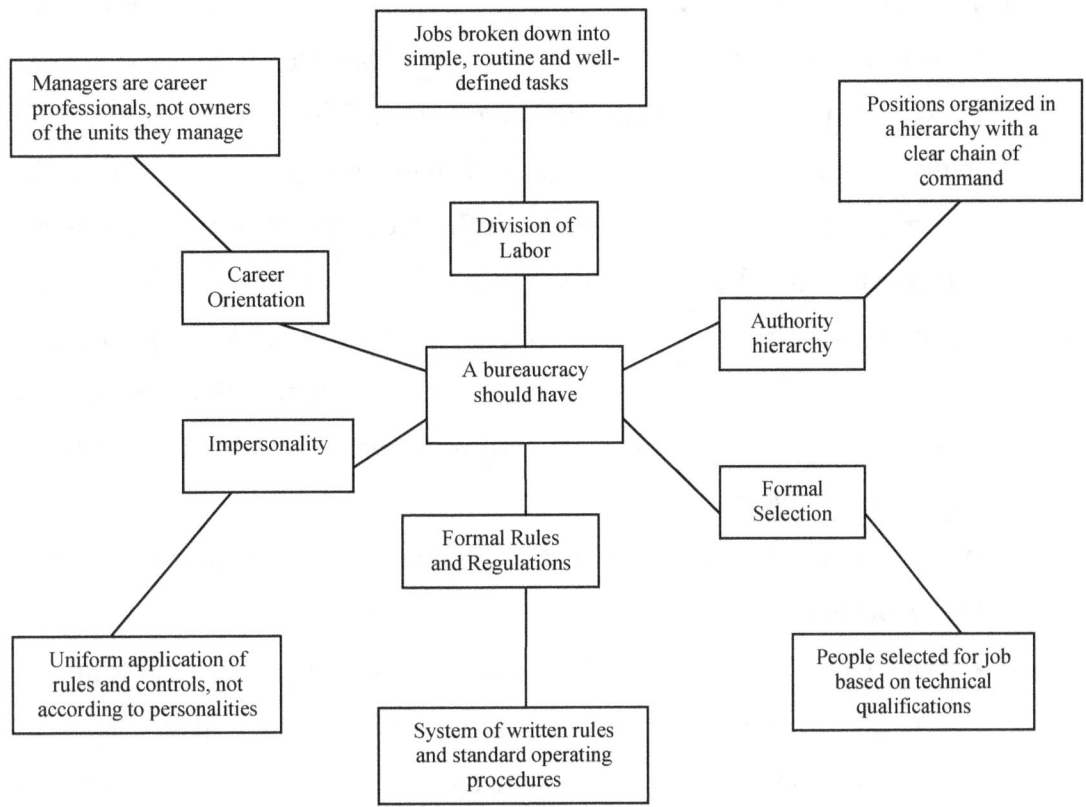

Figure-2.3 WEBER'S IDEAL BUREAUCRACY

The Elements of Bureaucracy are:

- Labour is divided with clear definition of authority and responsibility that are legitimatized as official duties.
- Positions are organized in a hierarchy of authority, with each position under the authority of a higher one.
- All personnel are selected and promoted based on technical qualifications, which are assessed by examination or according to training and experience.
- Administrative acts and decisions are recorded in writing. Recordkeeping provides organizational memory and continuity over time.
- Management is separate from the ownership of the organization.
- Management is subject to rules and procedures that will insure reliable, predictable behaviour. Rules are impersonal and uniformly applied to all employees.

III **James D. Mooney and Alan C. Reilly:** James Mooney was a General Motors executive who teamed-up with historian Alan Reilly to expose the true principles of an organization in their books. They wrote a book 'Onward Industry' in 1931 and later revised and renamed it as 'Principles of Organization' which had greatly influenced the theory and practice of management in USA at that time. They contended that an efficient organization should be based on certain formal principles and premises. They contended that organizations should be studied from two view points:

(A) The employees who create and utilize the process of organization; and

(B) The objective of the process

With respect to first aspect, their contributions to some fundamental principles of organization are:

- The Coordination Principle: It was considered to be the single basic principle that actually encompassed the other two principles. They defined coordination as the orderly arrangement of work group effort that provides unity of action in pursuit of common goals.

- The Scalar Principle: It was borrowed from the Fayol's work, was the devise for grading duties in accordance with the amount of authority possessed at the different organizational levels.

- The Functional Principle: The functional distinction is those unique differences in organizational operations that the manager must perceive in order to effectively integrate and coordinate all the functions of the organization.

In essence, Mooney and Reilley made an attempt to offer a rigid framework of management theory with emphasis on hierarchical structure, clear division and definition of authority and responsibility, specialization of tasks, coordination of activities and utilization of staff experts.

IV **Chester Barnard (1886-1961):** Chester Barnard, president of Bell Telephone Company, developed theories about the functions of the manager as determined by constant interaction with the environment. Barnard saw organizations as social systems that require human cooperation. He expressed his view in his book *The Function of the Executive*. He proposed ideas that bridged classical and human resource view points. Barnard believes that organizations were made up of people with interacting social relationships. The manager's major functions were to communicate and stimulate subordinates to high level of efforts.

He saw the effectiveness of an organization as being dependent on its ability to achieve cooperative efforts from a number of employees in a total, integrated system. Barnard also argued that success depended on maintaining good relations with the people and institutions with whom the organization regularly interacted. By recognizing the organization's dependence on investors, suppliers, customers, and other external stakeholders, Barnard introduced the idea that managers had to examine the external environment and then adjust the organization to maintain a state of equilibrium. Barnard also developed set of working principles by which organizational communication systems can maintain final authority for the management team. These principles are:

- Channels of communication should be definitely known.
- Objective authority requires a definite formal channel of communication to every members of an organization.
- The line of communication must be as direct or short as possible.
- The complete line of communication should usually be used.
- Competence of the persons serving at communication centers that is officers, supervisory heads, must be adequate.
- The line of communication should not be interrupted during the time the organization is to function.

V **Herbert A. Simon**: Simon, the Noble Laureate in economics (1978), is an American political and social scientist. He started his career in local government. He analyzed the classical principles of management. Due to their ambiguous and contradictory nature, he criticized these principles as 'myths'. He analyzed the problems of management from the socio-psychological view point. But he is best known for his work in the field of decision making and administrative behaviour. He perceived the modern manager as being limited in his knowledge of a problems and the number of alternative available to him is also limited. Thus, the manager is an administrative man, not an economic man, who makes decision amid bounded rationality and selects not the maximizing alternative. Simon's arguments for the administrative man concept of a manager are highlighted in *Table-2.3*:

TABLE-2.3 ECONOMIC MAN AND ADMINISTRATIVE MAN

Economic Man- Full Rationality	**Administrative Man-Bounded Rationality**
1. Economic man maximizes- selects the best alternative from among all those available to him.	Administrative man satisfies- looks for a course of action that is satisfactory or good enough.
2. Economic man deals with the real world in all its complexity. He is rational.	Administrative man recognizes that the world he perceives is a drastically simplified model of the buzzing, blooming confusion that constitute the real world.
3. Rationality requires a complete knowledge and anticipation of the consequences that will follow on each choice.	Knowledge of consequences is always fragmentary. Since these consequences lies in the future, imaginations must supply the lack of experienced feeling.
4. Rationality requires a choice among all possible alternative behaviour.	In actual behaviour only a very few of all possible alternatives ever come to mind.

(C) **Behavioural School:** The school of behavioural management theory involved in recognition on the importance of human behaviour in organization. The major contributors were *Figure-2.4*:

I. **Robert Owen (1771-1858)** was a British industrialist who was the first to speak out on behalf of the organization's human resources. He carried out experiments and introduced many social reforms. He believed that workers' performance was influenced by the total environment in which they worked. He criticized industrialists who spent huge sums of money repairing their production machines, but did little to improve the lot of their human machines. Owen worked for the building up of a spirit of co-operation between the workers and managers. He introduced new ideas of human relations e.g. shorter work hours, housing facilities, education of children, provision of canteen, training of workers in hygiene etc. He suggested that proper treatment of workers pays dividends and is an essential part of every manager's job.

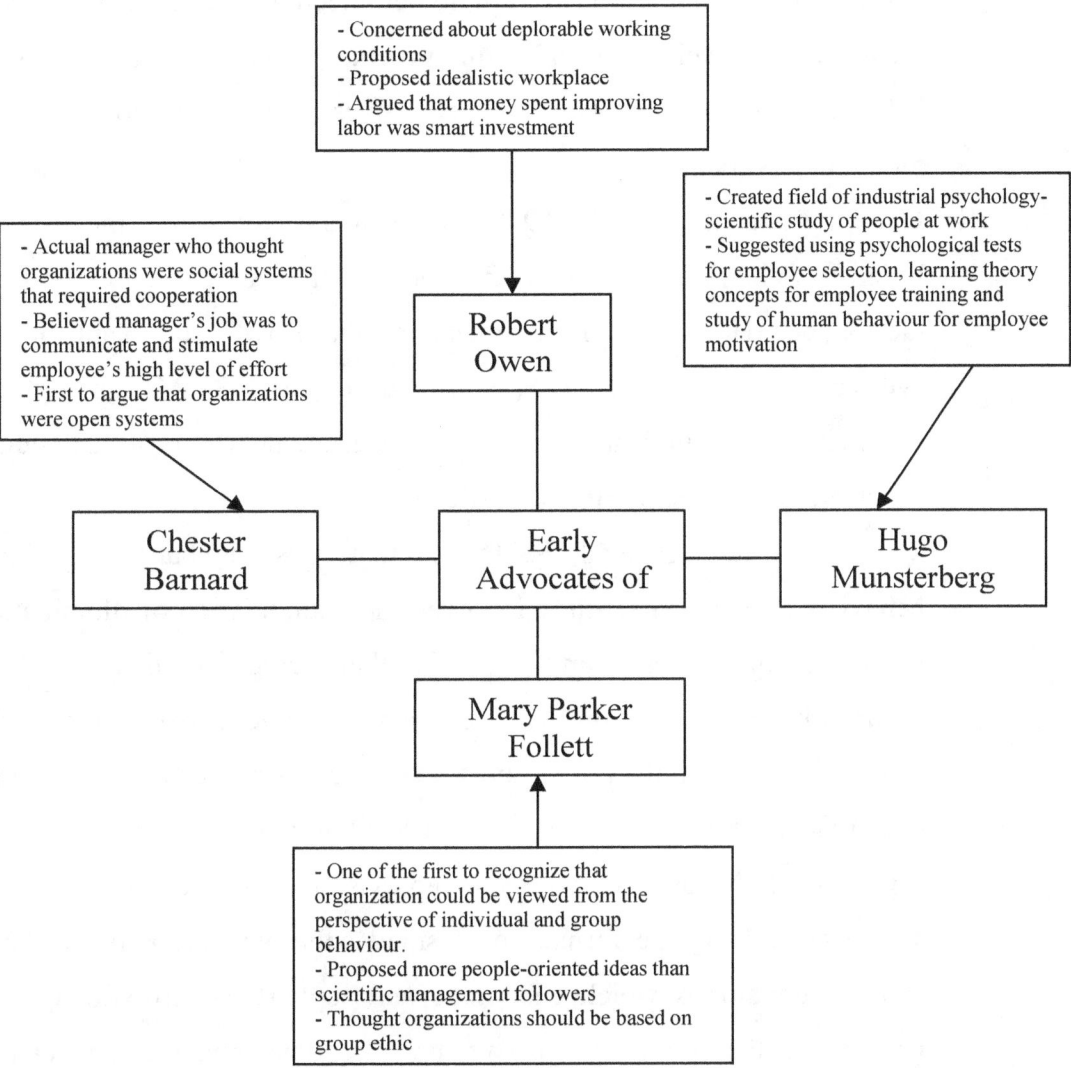

Figure-2.4 EARLY ADVOCATES OF ORGANIZATION BEHAVIOUR

II. **Hugo Munsterberg (1863-1916):** developed a psychology laboratory at Harvard University where he studied the application of psychology to the organizational settings. Psychology and Industrial Efficiency he argued for the study of scientific study of human behaviour to identify the general patterns and to explain individual differences. Thus, his concern for the human side of business led his peers to consider him to be father of industrial psychology. He successfully documented the psychological conditions associated with varying levels of work productivity, and he instructed managers on ways to match workers with jobs and also how to motivate them. Munsterberg suggested the use of psychological tests to improve employee selection, the value of learning theory in the development of training methods, and the study of human behaviour to determine what techniques are most effective for motivating workers.

III. **George Elton Mayo (1880-1949):** Mayo was a professor at the Harvard Business School. He served as the leader of the team which carried out the famous Hawthorne Experiments at the Hawthorne plant of the Western Electric Company (USA) during 1927-32. Originally the research was an application of Taylor's management science techniques designed to improve production efficiency.

Mayo discussed in detail the factors that cause a change in human behaviour. Mayo's first study involved the manipulation of illumination for one group of workers and comparing their output with that of another group whose illumination was held constant. He concluded that the cause of increase in the productivity of workers is not a single factor like changing working hours or rest pauses but a combination of these several other factors. Considerate supervision, giving autonomy to the workers, allowing the formation of small cohesive groups of workers, creating conditions which encourage and support the growth of these groups and the cooperation between workers and management lead to increase in productivity.

Mayo's contribution to management thoughts lies in the recognition of the fact that worker's performance is related to psychological, sociological and physical factors. Mayo and his associates concluded that a new social setting created by their tests had accounted for the increase in productivity. Their finding is now known as the Hawthorne Effect or the tendency for people, who are singled out for special attention, to improve their performance. Hawthorne study was an important landmark in studying the behaviour of workers and his relationship to the job, his fellow workers and organization. He highlighted that workers were found to restrict their output in order to avoid displeasure of the group, even at the sacrifice of incentive pay. Thus, Hawthorne studies were a milestone in establishing the framework for further studies into the field of organizational behaviour.

IV. **Mary Parker Follett (1868-1933):** She was a social philosopher whose ideas had clear implications for management practice. Her contribution towards the understanding of group is of immense value. She believed that groups were the mechanisms through which people could combine their differing talents for the greater good of the organization, which she defined as the community in which managers and subordinates could work in harmony. The Mangers and workers should view themselves as partners and as a part of common group. She was convicted that the traditional and artificial distinction between the managers who give the orders and the workers who take the orders obscured their natural relationships. Manager should rely more on their expertise and knowledge to lead subordinates than on the formal authority of their position. Thus, her humanistic ideas influenced the way we look at motivation, leadership, power and authority. The Follett Behavioural Model of control being sponsored by an oriented towards the group, while self-control exercised by both individuals and the group ultimately result in both sharing the power. In the Follett Holistic Model of Control, Follett captured the interactive, integrative nature of self-control groups being influenced by the forces within the work environment.

V. **Abraham Maslow**: He was a humanistic psychologist, proposed a hierarchy of five needs: physiological, safety, social, esteem and self-actualization. He proposed that man was a wanting animal whose behaviour was calculated to serve his most pressing needs. A need can be described as a physiological or psychological deficiency that a person is motivated to satisfy. Maslow further proposed that man's need could be placed in a hierarchy of needs as shown in *Figure-2.5*. The study shows that a man has various needs and their order can be determined. The moment the first need of man is satisfied he starts thinking of the second need, and then follows his worry about the third need and the sequence continues till all the needs are satisfied. Maslow's theory is operationalized through two principles.

- The *deficit principle* holds that a relatively well-satisfied need is not a strong motivator of behaviour.
- The *progression principle* holds that, once a need is fairly-well satisfied, behaviour is dominated by the next level in the need hierarchy.

1) Physiological Needs: This category includes those needs which a man needs to satisfy first of all in order to remain alive. It includes food to eat, house to live in, clothes to wear and sleep for rest.

2) Safety Needs: After having satisfied the physical needs a man thinks of his safety. Safety needs mean physical, economic and psychological safety. *Physical safety* means saving him from accidents, diseases and other unforeseen situations. *Economic safety* means security of employment and making provision for old age. *Psychological safety* means maintaining his prestige.

3) Social Needs: Man is a social being and wants to live in society with honour. It is, therefore, necessary that he should have friends and relatives with whom he can share his joys and sorrows.

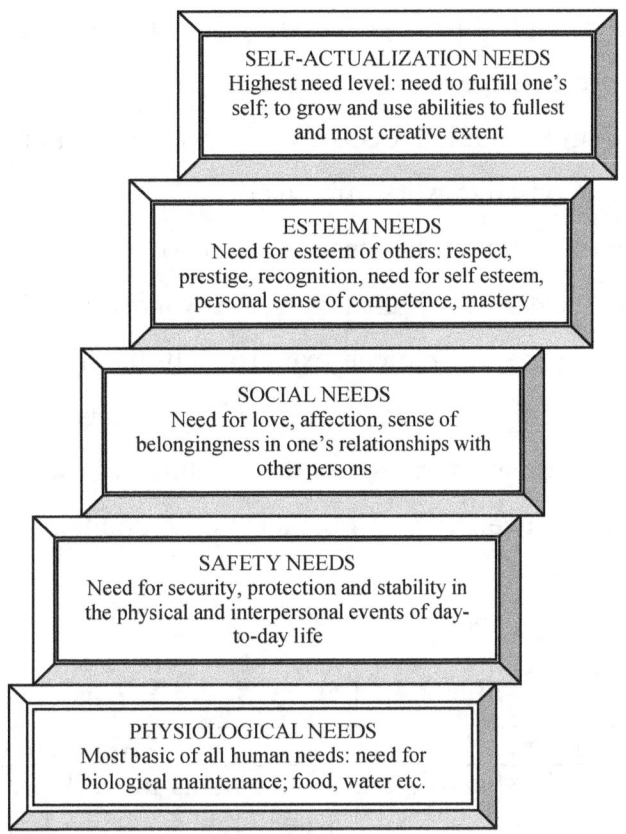

Figure-2.5 MASLOW'S HIERARCHY OF HUMAN NEEDS

    4) Esteem and Status Needs: They are called ego needs of man. It means everybody wants to get a high status which may increase his power and authority.

    5) Self Actualization Needs: Last of all man tries to satisfy his self actualization need. It means that a man should become what he is capable of. For example- a musician wants to be proficient in the art of music, an artist wants to gain proficiency in creating works of art and similarly, a poet wants to be an expert in the art of writing poems.

VI. **Douglas McGregor (1906-1964):** He is best known for his formulation of two sets of assumptions- Theory X and Theory Y. McGregor argued that managers should shift their traditional views of man and work (which he termed Theory X) to a new humane views of man and work (which he termed Theory Y).

According to McGregor, Theory X attitudes, that man was lazy and work was bad were both pessimistic and counter productive. Theory X assumes that people have little ambition, dislike work, want to avoid responsibility, and need to be closely supervised to work effectively.

Theory Y, view that man wanted to work and work was good should become the standard for humanizing the workplace. Theory Y offers a positive view, assuming that people can exercise self-direction, accept responsibility and consider work to be as natural as rest of play. McGregor believed that Theory Y assumptions best captured the true nature of workers and should guide management practice. *Table-2.4* depicts the assumptions of both these theories:

Table-2.4: Theory X and Y Theory

Traditional Theory 'X'	**Modern Theory 'Y'**
1) Man by nature is sluggish and shirker.	Man wants to work provided the conditions are favourable.
2) Mostly people are not ambitious and are afraid to take responsibility.	This theory takes people as enthusiastic, responsible and full of effort.
3) Under this people want to be directed, meaning thereby that they want somebody to tell them to work and only they will work.	It is thought that the employee has the quality of self-direction and they do not feel the necessity of being directed by somebody else.
4) Motivation is limited to only physical and security needs.	According to this, physical and security needs motivate for a short time while it is continuous in case of self-actualization and esteem and status needs.
5) Strict control, threat and punishment are used in order to get work.	If proper environment is provided a person himself performs his work laboriously.

VII. **Chris Argyris:** He was an eminent social scientist and a professor of industrial administration at Yale University. He conducts research into personality and organizational life factors and developed the theory that both traditional management practices and organizational structure are inconsistent with the growth and development of the matured personality. Further he argued that the continuing incongruence between one's work environment and one's personality will result in conflict, frustration and failure.

(D) **Quantitative School:** With the revolutionary change in the application of information technology came the quantitative school of thoughts, which finds its foundation in decision theory, the application of statistics in decision making and the evolution of mathematical/econometric models that are nurtured by computer technology. This approach is based upon the assumption that mathematical techniques can help the manager in solution of problems. The features of quantitative management school were:

- Primary Focus on Decision Making: The end result of problem analysis will include direct implications for managerial action.
- Based on Economic Decision Theory: Final actions are chosen criteria as costs, revenue and rates of return on investment.
- Use of Formal Mathematical Models: Possible solutions to problems are specified as mathematical equations and then analyzed according to mathematical rules and formulas.
- Frequent Use of Computers: Heavy reliance is placed on computers and their advanced processing capabilities.

The quantitative approach has found favor through the following applications:

I. Management Science: Explained later in this chapter.

II. Operations Management: It entails the application of quantitative methods to the organizational tasks of production and operations control. The operational management techniques utilizes following basic quantitative techniques:

- *Forecasting* is the process by which future predictions are formulated through mathematical computations
- *Inventory control* entails the control of costly inventories through mathematical formulas that determine the proper level of

inventory to be maintained as well as the economic quantities to be ordered.

- *Linear programming* involves the use of computations to allocate scarce resources for their optimal use.

- *Networks* are complex models, such as Program Evaluation and Review Techniques (PERT) and the Critical Path Methods (CPM) for analyzing, planning and controlling complex operations.

- *Regression analysis* is used to predict the relationships between two or more variables and to determine how changes in one variable might affect other variables.

III. Management Information System: These are integrated programs for the collection, analysis and dissemination of information to support management decision making. The total MIS network is more than a machine; it contains human resources, hardware, software and intricate processes. Most MIS networks are computer based due to vast amount of number crunching to be done. That is why the ideal MIS provides accurate, condensed informational analysis to the appropriate manager in a timely manner.

2. Integration School

In recent years, an attempt has been made to integrate the classical theories with the modern behavioural and quantitative theories into an overall framework that use the best of each approach. These approaches assumed that there is no best way to manage, and all theories have application to the practice of management. Two such integrative developments are explained as follows:

I. **Contingency Theory**: It is based on the notion that the proper management technique in a given situation depends upon the nature and conditions of that situation. The contingency view of management is highlighted in *Figure-2.6* contend that an organizational phenomenon exists in logical patterns which managers can come to understand. Along with this organizational understanding comes the development of unique behaviours that have proven successful in particular situations. However, there are no universal solution techniques because every problem situation is unique in itself.

Figure-2.6 THE CONTINGENCY VIEW OF MANAGEMENT

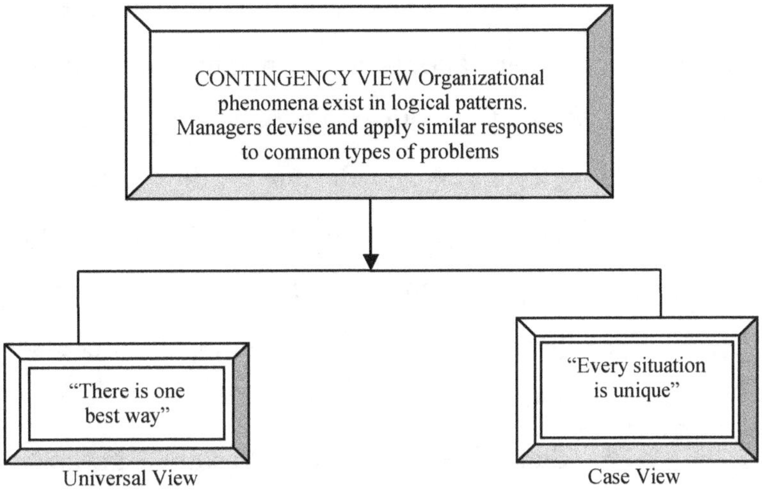

```
        ┌─────────────────────────────────────┐
        │ CONTINGENCY VIEW Organizational     │
        │ phenomena exist in logical patterns.│
        │ Managers devise and apply similar   │
        │ responses to common types of        │
        │ problems                            │
        └─────────────────────────────────────┘
                         │
            ┌────────────┴────────────┐
            ▼                         ▼
    ┌───────────────┐         ┌───────────────┐
    │ "There is one │         │ "Every        │
    │  best way"    │         │  situation    │
    │               │         │  is unique"   │
    └───────────────┘         └───────────────┘
       Universal View              Case View
```

II   **Systems Theory:** It has been explained later in this lesson.

3. ## Contemporary School

    The contemporary school of management thoughts outlines the framework for studying the more recent trends in management practices, such as the impact of global business, Theory Z concepts, McKinsey 7-S approach, the search for excellence, and the concern for quality and productivity. These are explained as follows:

    I   **Global:** The recent emergence of a truly global economy is affecting every manager in the world. In today's environment, success in the long run demands that the manager think globally, even if he can still limit his actions to local market.

    II   **Theory Z**: These firms are those which are highly successful American firms that use many of the Japanese management practices. The Type Z firm features long-term employment with a moderately specialized career path and slow evaluation and promotion. Lifetime employment would not be especially attractive to America's mobile work force and the slow evaluation and promotion processes would not meet the high expectations of American workers.

III **Mckinsey 7-S**: The 7-S factors are as follows:

- Strategy: The plans that determine the allocation of an organization's scarce resources and commit the organization to a specified course of action.
- Structure: The design of the organization that determines the number of levels in its hierarchy and the location of the organization's authority.
- Systems: The organizational processes and proceduralized reports and routines.
- Staff: The key human resource groups within an organization, described demographically.
- Style: The manner in which manager behave in pursuit of organizational goals.
- Skills: The distinct abilities of the organization's personnel.
- Super ordinate Goals (shared values): The significant meanings or guiding concepts that an organization instill in its members.

IV **Excellence**: The firms that qualified as excellent companies shared the following characteristics:

- A successful firm makes things happen.
- Successful firms make it a point to know their customers and their needs.
- Autonomy and Entrepreneurship is valued in each employee.
- Productivity through people is based on trust.
- Hands on, value driven management is mandatory.
- A firm must always deal with strength.
- A firm leads to cost effective works teams.
- A firm can decentralize many decisions while retaining tight controls, usually through the function of finance.

V **Quality and Productivity**: In today's dynamic marketplace, consumers are encouraged to buy a product that demonstrates the highest level of quality at the optimum price. This requires a dedicated and skilled work force that places utmost importance on quality workmanship.

2.5 APPROACHES TO THE STUDY OF MANAGEMENT

A. Classical Approach

The classical approach is also known as traditional approach, management process approach or empirical approach. The main features of this approach are as follows:

- It laid emphasis on division of labour and specialization, structure, scalar and functional processes and span of control. Thus, they concentrated on the anatomy of formal organization.

- Management is viewed as a systematic network (process) of interrelated functions. The nature and content of these functions, the mechanics by which each function is performed and the interrelationship between these function is the core of the classical approach.

- It ignored the impact of external environment on the working of the organization. Thus, it treated organization as closed system.

- On the basis of experience of practicing managers, principles are developed. These principles are used as guidelines for the practicing executive.

- Functions, principles and skills of management are considered universal. They can be applied in different situations.

- The integration of the organization is achieved through the authority and control of the central mechanism. Thus, it is based on centralization of authority.

- Formal education and training is emphasized for developing managerial skills in would be managers. Case study method is often used for this purpose.

- Emphasis is placed on economic efficiency and the formal organization structure.
- People are motivated by economic gains. Therefore, organization controls economic incentives.

The Classical approach was developed through three mainstreams- Taylor's Scientific Management, Fayol's Administrative Management and Weber's Ideal Bureaucracy. All the three concentrated on the structure of organization for greater efficiency.

Merits of Classical Approach

- The classical approach offers a convenient framework for the education and training of managers.
- The observational method of case study is helpful in drawing common principles out of past experience with some relevance for future application
- It focuses attention on what managers actually do.
- This approach highlights the universal nature of management.
- It provides scientific basis for management practice.
- It provides a starting point for researchers to verify the validity and to improve the applicability of management knowledge. Such knowledge about management is effectively presented.

Shortcomings of Classical Approach

- Weber's ideal bureaucracy suggested strict adherence to rules and regulations, this lead to redtapism in the organization.
- It offers a mechanistic framework that undermines the role of human factor. The classical writers ignored the social, psychological and motivational aspect of human behaviour.
- The environmental dynamics and their effect on management have been discounted. Classical theory viewed organization as closed system i.e. having no interaction with environment.

- There is positive danger in relying too much on past experiences because a principle or technique found effective in the past may not fit a situation of the future.
- The classical principles are mostly based on the personal experience and limited observations of the practitioners. They are not based on personal experience.
- The totality of real situation can seldom be incorporated in a case study.

B. Scientific Management Approach

The impetus for the scientific management approach came from the first industrial revolution. Because it brought about such an extraordinary mechanization of industry, this revolution necessitated the development of new management principles and practices. The concept of scientific management was introduced by Frederick Winslow Taylor in USA in the beginning of 20th century. He defined scientific management as," *Scientific management is concerned with knowing exactly what you want men to do and then see in that they do it in the best and cheapest way"*.

Elements and Tools of Scientific Management: The features of various experiments conducted by Taylor are as follows:

- *Separation of Planning and doing*: Taylor emphasized the separation of planning aspects from actual doing of the work. The planning should be left to the supervisor and the workers should emphasize on operational work.
- *Functional Foremanship*: Separation of planning from doing resulted into development of supervision system that could take planning work adequately besides keeping supervision on workers. Thus, Taylor evolved the concept of functional foremanship based on specialization of functions. This involve activities of workers as depicted in Figure-2.7:

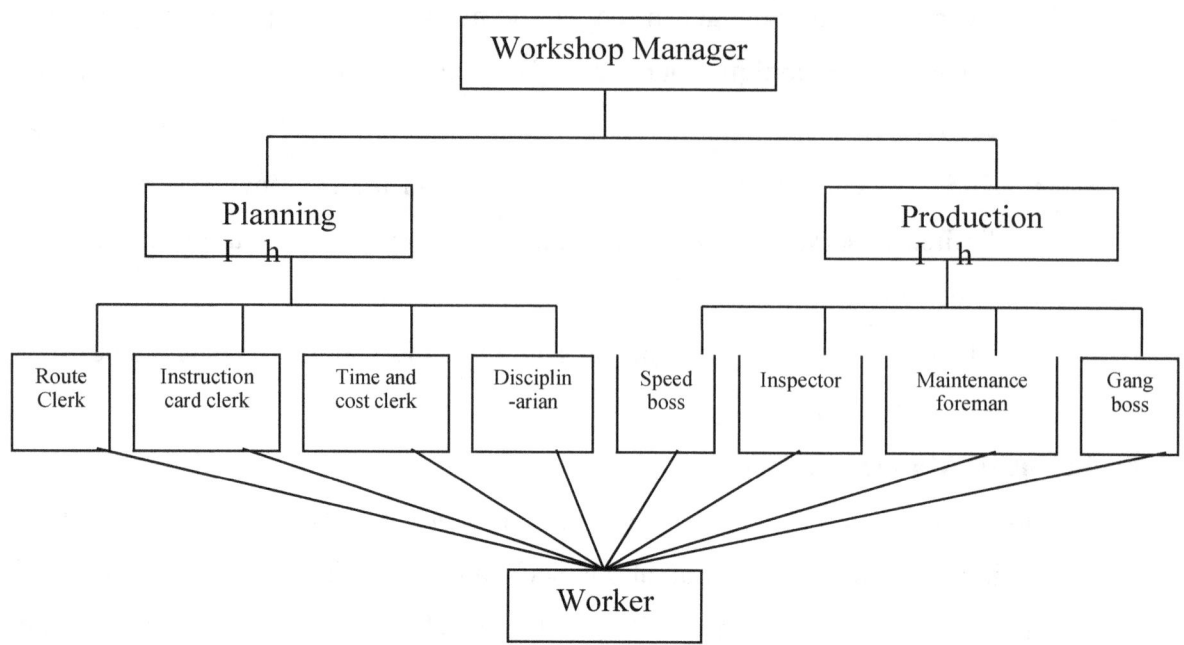

Figure-2.7 FUNCTIONAL FOREMANSHIP

- *Job Analysis*: It is undertaken to find out the best way of doing things. The best way of doing a job is one which requires the least movement consequently less time and cost.

- *Standardization*: Standardization should be maintained in respect of instruments and tools, period of work, amount of work, working conditions, cost of production etc.

- *Scientific Selection and Training of Workers*: Taylor has suggested that the workers should be selected on scientific basis taking into account their education, work experience, aptitudes, physical strength etc.

- *Financial Incentives*: Financial incentives can motivate workers to put in their maximum efforts. Thus, monetary (bonus, compensation) incentives and non monetary (promotion, upgradation) incentives should be provided to employees.

Principles of Scientific Management: Already discussed in this lesson.

Criticism of Scientific Management: The main grounds of criticism are given below:

- Taylor advocated the concept of functional foremanship to bring about specialization in the organization. But this is not feasible in practice as a worker can't carry out instructions from eight foremen.
- Workers were hired on a first-come, first-hired basis without due concern for workers ability or skills.
- Scientific management is production oriented as it concentrates too much on the technical aspects of work and undermines the human factors in industry. It resulted in monotony of job, loss of initiative, over speeding workers, wage reductions etc.
- Training was haphazard at best, with only minimal use of basic apprentice system.
- Tasks were accomplished by general rule of thumb without standard times, methods or motion.
- Managers worked side-by-side with the workers, often ignoring such basic managerial function of planning and organizing.

C. Administrative Approach to Management

The advocates of this school perceive management as a process involving certain functions such as planning, organizing, directing and controlling. That's why it is called as 'functional approach' or 'management process' approach. Fayol's contributions were first published in book form titled 'Administration Industrielle at Generale' in French Language, in 1916. He defined management in terms of certain functions and then laid down fourteen principles of management which according to him have universal applicability. Thus, he was a pioneer in the field of management education. In brief, Fayol's views on management command acceptability even today because they are much in tune with the requirements of management in the present day world.

Fayol's General Principles of Management

- *Division of Work*: The object of division of work is to produce more and better work with the same effort. It is accomplished through reduction in the number of tasks to which attention and effort must be directed.

- *Authority and Responsibility*: Authority is defined as 'the right to command and the power to make oneself obeyed'. Responsibility coexists with authority and is its other side. Fayol made a distinction between official authority and personal authority, the latter stemming from the manager's own intelligence, integrity, experience, personality, knowledge and skills.

- *Discipline*: It implies respect for agreements designed to secure obedience. It must prevail throughout an organization to ensure its smooth functioning. Discipline requires clear and fair agreements, good supervision and judicious application of penalties.

- *Unity of Command*: Every employee should receive orders and instruction from only one superior and a subordinate should be accountable to only one superior.

- *Unity of Direction*: Each group of activities having one objective should be unified by having one plan and one head.

- *Subordination of Individual to General Interest*: The interest of any one employee or group of employees should not take precedence over the interests of the organization as a whole.

- *Remuneration of Personnel*: The amount of remuneration and the methods of payment should be just and fair and should provide maximum possible satisfaction to both employees and employers.

- *Centralisation*: It refers to the degree to which subordinates are involved in decision making. Whether decision making is centralized (to management) or decentralized (to subordinates) is a question of proper proportion. The task is to find the optimum degree of centralization for each situation.

- *Scalar Chain*: The scalar chain is the chain of superiors ranging from the ultimate authority to the lowest ranks. Communication should follow this chain. However, if following the chain creates delays, cross-communications can be followed if agreed to by all parties and superiors are kept informed.

- *Order*: It is a rational arrangement for things and people. Fayol emphasized both material order and human order. In material order, there should be a place for everything and everything should be in its proper place. In human order, there should be an appointed place for everyone and everyone should be in his and her appointed place.
- *Equity*: Managers should be kind and fair to their subordinates. The application of equity requires good sense, experience and humanistic attitude for soliciting loyalty and devotion from subordinates.
- *Stability of Tenure*: High employee turnover is inefficient. Management should provide orderly personnel planning and ensure that replacements are available to fill vacancies.
- *Initiative*: Subordinates should be provided with an opportunity to show their initiative as a way to increase their skills and to inculcate a sense of participation.
- *Espirit de Corps*: Union is strength, and it comes from the harmony and mutual understanding of the personnel. Management should not follow the policy of 'divide and rule'. Rather it should strive to maintain team spirit and co-operation among employees so that they can work together as a team for the accomplishment of common objectives.

Criticism: Fayol's work has been criticized on the following grounds:

- His theory is said to be too formal. There is no single classification of managerial functions acceptable to all the functional theorists. There is also lack of unanimity about the various terms such as management, administration etc.
- He did not pay adequate attention to workers.
- The fundamentalists considered their principles to be universal in nature. But many of the principles have failed to deliver the desired results in certain situations.
- There is a vagueness and superficiality about some of his terms and definition.

TABLE-2.5 DISSIMILARITY BETWEEN CONTRIBUTION OF TAYLOR AND FAYOL

Basis of Comparison	Taylor	Fayol
1. Perspective	Shop floor level or the job of a supervisor	Top Management
2. Focus	Improving productivity through work simplification and standardization	Improving overall administration through general principles
3. Personality	Scientists	Practitioner
4. Results	Scientific observation and measurement	Universal Truths developed from personal experiences
5. Major Contribution	Science of industrial management	A systematic theory of management

D. Human Relation Approach to Management

The criticism of the Scientific and Administrative Management as advocated by Taylor and Fayol, respectively, gave birth to Human Relation Approach. The behavioural scientists criticized the early management approaches for their insensitiveness to the human side of organization. The behavioural scientists did not view the employees mechanically in work situation, but tried to show that the employees not only have economic needs but also social and psychological needs like need for recognition, achievement, social contact, freedom, and respect. Human relations school regards business organization as a psycho-social system.

Elton Mayo of Harvard and his associates conducted a famous study on human behaviour at the Hawthorne plant of the Western Electric Company and this study formed the foundation of this school of management thoughts. The basic hypotheses of this study as well as the basic propositions of the Human Relation Approach are the following:

- The business organization is a social system.
- The employees not only have economic needs but also psychological needs and social needs, which are required to be served properly to motivate them.
- Employees prefer self-control and self-direction.

- Employee oriented democratic participative style of management is more effective than mechanistic task oriented management style.
- The informal group should be recognized and officially supported.

The human relations approach is concerned with recognition of the importance of human element in organizations. It revealed the importance f social and psychological factors in determining worker's productivity and satisfaction. It is instrumental in creating a new image of man and the work place. However, this approach also did not go without criticism. It was criticized that the approach laid heavy emphasis on the human side as against the organizational needs. However, the contribution of this approach lies in the fact that it advises managers to attach importance to the human side of an organization.

E. Social System Approach to Management

It is developed during social science era, is closely related to Human Relation Approach. It includes those researchers who look upon management as a social system. Chester I. Barnard is called as the spiritual father of this approach. According to this approach, an organization is essentially a cultural system composed of people who work in cooperation. The major features of this approach are as follows:

- Organization is a social system, a system of cultural relationships.
- Relationships exist among the external as well as internal environment of the organization.
- Cooperation among group members is necessary for the achievement of organizational objectives.
- For effective management, efforts should be made for establishing harmony between the goals of the organization and the various groups therein.

F. Decision Theory Approach to Management

Decision Theory is the product of management science era. The decision theorists emphasize on rational approach to decisions, i.e. selecting from possible alternatives a course of action or an idea. Major contribution in this approach has come from Simon. Other contributors are March, Cyert, Forrester etc. The major emphasis of this approach is that decision making is the job of every manager. The manager is a decision maker and the organization is a decision making unit. Therefore, the major problem of managing is to make rational decision. The main features of this approach are:

- Management is essentially decision-making. The members of the organization are decision makers and problem solvers.
- Organization can be treated as a combination of various decision centers. The level and importance of organizational members are determined on the basis of importance of decisions which they make.
- All factors affecting decision making are subject matter of the study of management. Thus, it covers the entire range of human activities in organization as well as the macro conditions within which the organization works.

G. Management Science Approach to Management

Management science is an approach to management that applies mathematical analysis to decision making. It involves the use of highly sophisticated techniques, statistical tools and complex models. The primary focus of this approach is the mathematical model. Through this device, managerial and other problems can be expressed in basic relationships and where a given goal is sought, the model can be expressed in terms which optimize that goal. The management science approach found its origins during World War II, when highly technical military/production problems become far too complex for traditional management methodology. The major features of this approach are:

- Management is regarded as the problem-solving mechanism with the help of mathematical tools and techniques.

- Management problems can be described in terms of mathematical symbols and data. Thus every managerial activity can be quantified.
- This approach covers decision making, system analysis and some aspect of human behaviour.
- Operations research, mathematical tools, simulation, model etc, are the basic methodologies to solve managerial problems.

H. Human Behavioural Approach to Management

Human Behavioural approach is a modified version of Human Relation approach. Human Behavioural approach is devoid of any emotional content, which is the core of Human Relation Approach. This approach stresses the individual performing the jobs. Here the attention is directed towards the human aspects of management. The neglect of human factor and the over emphasis on machines and materials led to the development of this approach. The Behavioural approach emphasizes synchronization of group goals within the broader framework of management. It does not consider the goals of the different groups as conflicting with others.

Many sociologists, psychologists and social psychologists have shown considerable interest in studying the problems of management. The sociologists who have contributed to management are Blak, Selznick, Homans, Dubin, Dalton, and Katz and Kahn. The social psychologist who have contributed to management are McGregor, Argyris, Leavitt, Blake and Mouton, Sayles, Tannenbaum and his associates, Bennis, Fielder, Stogdill and Herzberg. The behavioural theories have drawn heavily on the work of Maslow. Douglas McGregor built on Maslow's work in explaining his 'Theory X' and 'Theory Y'. Frederick Herzberg develops a two factor theory of motivation. To sum up, many conclusions of the contributions made by behaviouralists can presented as follows:

- People do not dislike work. If they have helped to establish objectives, they want to achieve them. In fact, job itself is a source of motivation and satisfaction to employees.

- Most people can exercise a great deal of self-direction and self-control than are required in their current job. Therefore, there remains untapped potential among them.
- The manager's basic job is to use the untapped human potential in the service organization.
- The managers should create a healthy environment wherein all the subordinates contribute to the best of their capacity. Te environment should provide healthy, safe, comfortable and convenient place to work.
- The manager should provide for self direction by subordinates and they must be encouraged to participate fully in all important matters.
- Operating efficiency can be improved by expanding subordinate influence, direction and self control.
- Work satisfaction may improve as a by product of subordinates making use of their potential.

Merits of Behavioural Approach

It generated an awareness of the overwhelming role of the human element in organizations. It recognizes the quality of leadership as a critical factor in management success. It recognizes the role of individual psychology and group behaviour in organizational effectiveness.

Shortcomings of Behavioural Approach

Conclusions of behavioural approach discounts theory and stress radical empiricism. This approach neglects the economic dimension of work satisfaction. It is group oriented and anti-individualistic.

TABLE-2.6 DISTINCTION BETWEEN HUMAN RELATIONS AND BEHAVIOURAL APPROACH

Human Relations Approach	Behavioural Sciences Approach
1. It laid emphasis on individual, his needs and behaviour.	It stressed upon groups and group behaviour.
2. It focused on inter-personal relationships	It focused on group relationships.
3. It was based on the Hawthorne Experiments and so its scope is limited.	It refined the Human Relations approach and has a wide scope. It is much more systematic study of human behaviour in organization.
4. It was pioneered by Elton Mayo and its associates.	It was pioneered by Feith Davis, Rensis Likert and others.
5. It laid emphasis on informal groups' motivation, job satisfaction and morale.	The behaviourists studied group dynamics, informal organization leadership. Motivation and participative management.

I. Mathematics or Quantitative Approach to Management

It emphasizes that the organization or decision making is a logical process and it can be expressed in terms of mathematical symbols and relationships, which can be used to solve corporate problems and conduct corporate affairs. This approach focuses attention on the fundamentals of analysis and decision making. This brings together the knowledge of various disciplines like Operation Research and Management Science for effective solution of management problems. The Quantitative School quantifies the problem; generate solution, tests the solution for their optimality and then it recommends. The decisions are optimum and perfect as distinguished from the human behavioural approach, in which decisions are 'satisfying'. This approach is devoid of any personal bias, emotions, sentiments, and intuitiveness. The main postulates of the quantitative approach are as follows:

- Management is a series of decision making. The job of a manager is to secure the best solution out of a series of interrelated variables.
- These variables can be presented in the form of a mathematical model. It consists of a set of functional equation which set out the quantitative interrelationship of the variable.

- If the model is properly formulated and the equations are correctly solved, one can secure the best solution to the model.
- Organizations exist for the achievement of specific and measurable economic goals.
- In order to achieve these goals, optimal decisions must be made through scientific formal reasoning backed by quantification.
- Decision making models should be evaluated in the light of set criteria like cost reduction, return on investment, meeting time schedules etc.
- The quality of management is judged by the quality of decisions made in diverse situations.

TABLE-2.7 DIFFERENCE BETWEEN QUANTITATIVE APPROACH AND SCIENTIFIC APPROACH

Quantitative Approach	Scientific Management
1. It makes use of mathematical and statistical techniques in management.	It makes use of scientific approach in management.
2. It focuses on finding right answers to managerial problems (decision making).	It focuses on improving efficiency of men and machines (one best way of doing things).
3. In this operation research is the main techniques	Time and motion studies are the main techniques.
4. It is developed by W. C. Churchman.	A movement launched by F. W. Taylor and his associates.
5. Application of Econometric models.	Application of Experiments and research.

J. System Approach to Management

In the 1960s, a new approach to management appeared which attempted to unify the earlier school of thoughts. This approach is commonly referred to as 'System Approach'. The system approach is based on the generalization that an organization is a system and its components are inter-related and inter-dependent. "A system is composed of related and dependent elements which, when in interactions, form a unitary whole. On other words, a system may be defined as an organized and purposeful entity of inter-related, inter-dependent and inter-acting elements. It is a goal oriented organism that is composed of parts interrelated in such a way that the total system is greater than the sum of its parts. The elements of each system may themselves be sub systems. These sub-systems are functionally related to each other and to the total system. The basic postulates of the system approach are as follows:

- An organization is a system consisting of several subsystems. For example, in a business enterprise production, sales and other departments re the subsystem
- The position and function of each subsystem can be analyzed only in relation to other subsystem and to the organization as a whole rather than in isolation.
- An organization is a dynamic system because it is responsive or sensitive to its environment. It is vulnerable to changes in its environment.

FIGURE: 2.8 OPEN SYSTEM VIEW OF ORGANIZATION

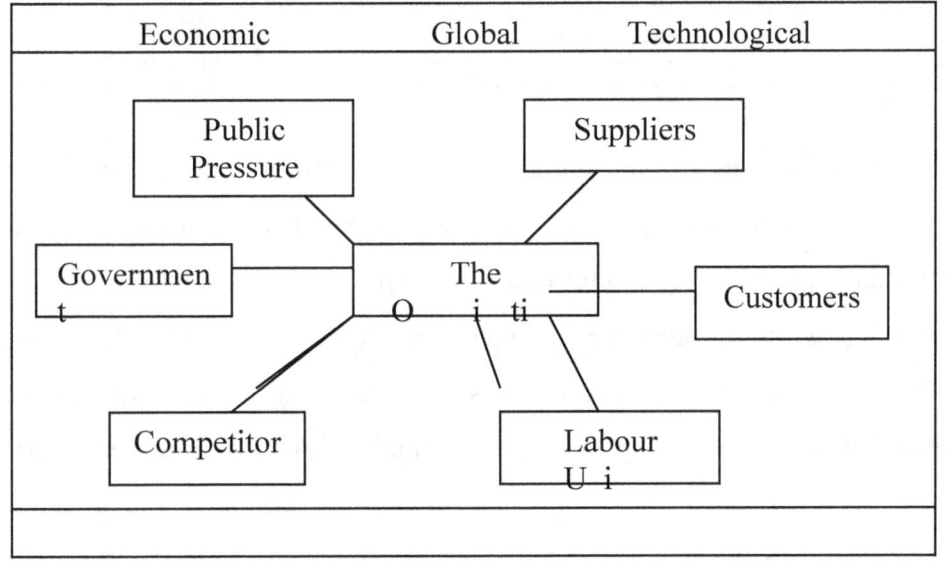

Systems are of several types. A *static system*, e.g. a petrol engine operates repetitively completing the same cycle of functions without change or deviation. On the other hand, the *dynamic system*, undergoes change, it grows or decays. Biological systems, e.g., plants, animals and human being are dynamic. A *closed system* is self-dependent and does not have any interaction with the external environment. Physical and mechanical systems are closed systems. A closed system concentrates completely on internal relationships, i.e. interaction between sub-systems only. An *open system* approach recognizes the dynamic interaction of the system with its environment in *Figure-2.8*:

The open system consisting of four basic elements

- Inputs: These are ingredients required to initiate the transformation process. They include human, financial, material and information resources.

Figure-2.9 ELEMENTS OF OPEN SYSTEM

Feedback from the environment

| Inputs from the environment: Material inputs, human inputs, financial inputs | → | Transformation process: Technology, operating systems, | → | Outputs into the environment: Products/services, profits/losses, employee behaviour, and |

- Transformation Process: The inputs are put through a transformation process that applies technology, operating methodologies, administrative practices and control techniques in order to produce the output.
- Outputs: The output may be products and/or services, the sale of which creates profits or losses. This process also has by-product outputs such as worker behaviour, information, environmental pollution, community services and so on.
- Feedback: A feedback loop is used to return the resultant environmental feedback to the system as inputs.

If the environment is satisfied with the output, business operations continue. If it is not, changes are initiated within the business systems so that requirements of the customers are fully met. This is how an open system responds to the forces of change in the environment.

K. Contingency or Situational Approach to Management

Another important approach which has arisen because of the inadequacy of the Quantitative, Behavioural and System Approach to management is the Contingency Approach. Pigors and Myers propagated this approach in 1950. Other contributors include Joan Woodward, Tom Burns, G.W.Stalker, Paul Lawrence, Jay Lorsch and James Thompson. They analyzed the relationship between organization and environment. They concluded that managers must keep the functioning of an organization in harmony with the needs of its members and the external forces. Management is situational and lies in identifying the important variables in a situation. The basic theme of contingency approach is that organizations have to cope with different situations in different ways. There cannot be particular management action which will be suitable for all situations. The management must keep the functioning of an organization in harmony with the needs of its members and the external forces.

According to Kast and Rosenzweig, "The contingency view seeks to understand the interrelationships within and among sub-system as well as between the organization and its environment and to define patterns of relationships or configurations of variables. Contingency views are ultimately directed towards suggesting organizational designs and managerial actions most appropriate for specific situations".

The approach has been used in important sub systems of management like organization, design, leadership, behaviour change and operation. The main features of contingency approach are:

- Management is entirely situational. The application and effectiveness of any techniques is contingent on the situation.
- Management action is contingent on certain action outside the system or subsystem as the case may be.
- Management should, therefore, match or fit its approach to the requirements of the particular situation. To be effective management policies and practices must respond to environmental changes.

- Organizational action should be based on the behaviour of action outside the system so that organization should be integrated with the environment.
- Management should understand that there is no one hard way to manage. They must not consider management principles and techniques universal.

A general framework for contingent management has been shown in the *Figure-2.10*. However, it is an abstract depiction of the contingency model. In order to operationalise the contingency approach, managers need to know the alternatives for different situations. It may be operationalized as a 'if then' approach to management. The environment (If) is an independent variable where as management (when) is a dependent variable. In this model, a manager has to take four sequential steps:

- Analyze and understand the situation,
- Examine the applicability or validity of different principles and techniques to the situation at hand,
- Make the right choice by matching the techniques to the situations,
- Implement the choice.

FIGURE-2.10 A CONCEPTUAL MODEL OF CONTINGENCY APPROACH

TABLE- 2.8 SYSTEM APPROACH VS. CONTINGENCY APPROACH

Systems Approach	Contingency Approach
1. It treats all organizations alike irrespective of their size, cultural settings and dynamics	It treats each organization as a unique entity.
2. It stresses interactions and interdependencies among systems and sub-systems.	It identifies the exact nature of inter dependencies and their impact on organizational design and managerial style.
3. It studies organization at an abstract and philosophical level.	It is more down to earth and action oriented.
4. It is neutral or non-committal on the validity of classical principles of management.	It firmly rejects the blind application of principles regardless of realities of individual situations.
5. It stresses upon the synergetic effect of organizations and the external input.	It is related to organization structure and design to the environment.
6. It is vague and complex.	It is pragmatic and action oriented.

2.6 SUMMARY

The study of organization and management is a must to understand the underlying principles of management. The foregoing analysis reveals that management thought is the outcome of diverse contributions of several management thinkers and practitioners. Each of this approach discussed above is an extension of the previous one. A composite or synthesis of various contributions made over a period of more than a century is the best management theory. The new trends, developments and challenges in the evolution of management thought and movement which will make new demands on managers in India are listed below:

- Growing intervention in trade, industry and commerce by the government. Growth of Trade Union Movement, profoundly influenced by political considerations only.
- Greater consciousness and growth of organizations of consumers.

- High cost economy and expansion of the services sector including the social sector, public sector and public utility services.
- Emerging growth of industry and consequent stiff competition from foreign goods, growth of multinational corporations in the context of new liberalized industrial policy.
- Rapid advancement in the field of technology.
- Utilization of information as an input and spread of Management Information System.
- Increasing Demand for participation by subordinates in decision making process. India is heading towards a business management manned by properly trained and educated persons.
- Social Responsibility and prevention of environmental pollution have aroused much public attention. This is indeed a great challenge to future and government is required to take necessary action in this regard.

TABLE-2. 9 SUMMARY OF APPROACHES AND CONTRIBUTIONS TO MANAGEMENT

Approach	Main Contributions	Main Contributors	Environment at that Time
Classical Approach	- Scientific Management - Management Functions - Administrative Theory - Bureaucracy	- F.W.Taylor, Frank Gilbreth, H. Emerson - Henery L. Gantt - L.F. Urwick, Mooney & Reliey, R.C.Davis - Max Weber	- Expanding Size of organization - Growing markets - Post-Industrial Revolution Decline of owner/ manager - Rise of professional manager
Behavioural Approach	- Human Relations - Hawthorne Experiments - Participation - MBO - Organizational Behaviour	- F.J. Roethlisberger - Elton Mayo - D. McGregor - P.F. Drucker - C.I. Barnard	- World War II unionization - Need for trained maangers - Government regulation - Labour unrest
Management Science Approach	- Operations Research - Simulation - Game Theory - Decision Theory - Mathematical Models	- W.C. Churchman - J.C. March - Forrester - H.A. Simon - Raiffa	- Cold war recession - Conglomerates - Indusrial/military conflict
System Approach	- Open System - Closed System - Socio-technical system	- E.L.Trist - A.K. Rice - F. E. Kast & J.E. Rosenzweig	- Turbulency - Information Technology - Robotics

	- Supra System - System interface mechanism	- R.A. Johnson - K.Boulding, D. Katz, R.L. Khan	- Pollution Problem
Contingency Approach	- Dynamic Environment - Organic mechanistic technology - Matrix designs and Social Responsibilities - Organizational Change - Information Systems	- Burns and Stalker - John Woodward - Thompson - P.R. Lawrence - J.A. Lorseh	- Space race. Expanding economy - High Technology - Global Trade - Social discontent - Rise of skilled professions

2.7 SELF ASSESSMENT EXERCISE

1. What are the some early evidences of management practice? Explain why division of labour and the industrial revolution are important to the study of management?

2. "F.W.Taylor is said to be the father of scientific management and Henri Fayol, the father of principles of management". Critically examine the statement.

3. Why is it important for every manager to understand the many different management theories that have been develop? Describe various School of Thoughts prevalent from time to time. Which school of management thoughts makes the most sense to you? Why?

4. Write a note on the evolution of management thought. What are the recent trends in management thoughts?

5. Write short note on the following:

    a) "Human Behavioural School of thought is a modified version of Human Relations School of thought". Comment.

    b) What is the System Approach to management? Explain the salient features of this approach.

6. Assess the role of following in development of management thoughts:

a) Henry Gantt

b) Weber

c) Maslow

d) Elton Mayo

2.8 SUGGESTED READINGS

1. Basu C. R., *Business Organization and Management*, 2nd Edition, Tata McGraw-Hill Ltd.
2. Brech, E. F. L., *Organization: The Framework of Management*, 2nd Edition, Longman.
3. Louis A. Allen, *Management and Organisation*, McGraw-Hill Kogakusha, Ltd.
4. Laurie J. Mullins, *Management and Organizational Behaviour*, Pitman.
5. Robbins Stephen P. and Mary Coulter, *Management*, 2002, Prentice Hall of India.
6. Robbins Stephen P. and Decenzo David A., *Fundamentals of Management*, 3rd Edition, Pearson Education Asia.

FUNCTIONS OF MANAGEMENT

Objective : The key objective of this lesson is to enable the students to understand the basic management functions along with their conceptual details.

Lesson Structure:

3.1 Introduction
3.2 Understanding Management as Concept
3.3 Functions of Management
    3.3.1 Planning
    3.3.2 Organizing
    3.3.3 Staffing
    3.3.4 Directing
    3.3.5 Coordinating
    3.3.6 Controlling
3.4 Summary
3.5 Self Assessment Questions
3.6 Suggested Readings

3.1 INTRODUCTION

Management practice is as old as human civilization, when people started living together in groups, for every human group requires management and the history of human beings is full of organizational activities. Even a smallest human group in our society i.e. family also needs management. The head of the family acts as top management and the housewife acts as a home manager. She plans about the work to be done, how the work has to be done, who is to do the work and whether the work is done properly or not. She performs all the four functions of management i.e. planning the budget and day to day activities, organizing the things and activities of different people, directing the servants and different members of the family and controlling activities of different members of the family. Family is a very informal type of human group. Even if this informal human group is not managed properly it will lead to great fuse and confusion. So, just imagine about large and complex institutions emerging these days.

During the last five decades, management as a discipline has attracted the attention of academicians and practitioners to a very great extent. The basic reason behind this phenomenon is the growing importance of management in day to day life of people. Today, the society has large and complex institutions with many people working together. The relationship between managers and managed has changed as compared to the older master-servant relationship making it more complex. People have greater expectations from their jobs. In order to make all these things function properly, people have been trying to evolve some method and techniques. Such attempts have given birth to management as a separate discipline. It has grown over the period of time making itself one of the most respected disciplines. Today, the study of management has become an important fact of human life.

3.2 UNDERSTANDING MANAGEMENT AS CONCEPT

The term management can have different meanings, and it is important to understand these different definitions. The term management can be considered as :-

1. **Management as a process :** Have you ever said "That is a well managed company" or "That organization has been mismanaged"? If you have, you seem to imply that : (i) management is some type of work or set of activities and (ii) sometimes the activities are performed quite well and sometimes not so well.

    You are referring to management as a process involving set of activities. Since the late nineteenth century, it has been common practice to define management in terms of four specific functions of managers. Planning, organizing, leading and controlling. We can thus say that management is the process of planning, organizing, leading and controlling the efforts of organization members and of using all other organizational resources to achieve stated organizational goals.

2. **Management as a discipline :** If you say you are a student of management or majoring in management, you are referring to the discipline of management. Classifying management as a discipline implies that it is an accumulated body of knowledge that can be learned. Thus management as a subject with principles, concepts and theories. A major purpose of studying the discipline of management is to learn and understand the principles, concepts, and theories of management and how to apply them in the process of managing.

3. **Management as people :** Whether you say, "That company has an entirely new management team" or "She is the best manager I have

ever worked for" you are referring to the people who guide, direct and thus, manage organizations. The word management used in this manner refers to the people, manager who engage in the process of management.

4. **Management as a career :** "Mr. Saxena has held several managerial positions since joining the bank upon his graduation from college". This statement implies that management is a career. People who devote their working lives to the process of management progress through a sequence of new activities and, often, new challenges. More than ever before, today's business environment is fast changing and competitive, posing challenges, opportunities, and rewards for individuals pursuing management as a career.

These different meanings of the term management has been related as follows by John M. Ivancevich -

"People who wish to have a career as a manager must study the discipline of management as a means toward practicing the process of management".

3.3. FUNCTIONS OF MANAGEMENT

Management process suggests that all the managers in the organization perform certain functions to get the things done by others. However, what are these functions which comprise management process is not quite clear and divergent views have been expressed on this. List of management functions varies from author to author with the number of functions ranging from three to eight.

There is enough disagreement among management writers on the classification of managerial functions. Newman and Summer recognize only four functions, namely, organizing, planning, leading and controlling. Henri Fayol identifies five functions of management, viz. planning, organizing, commanding, coordinating and controlling. Luther Gulick states seven such functions under the catch word "POSDCORB' which stands for planning, organizing, staffing, directing, coordinating, reporting and budgeting. Warren Haynes and Joseph Massie classify management functions into decision-making, organizing, staffing, planning, controlling, communicating and directing. Koontz and O'Donnell divide these functions into planning organizing, staffing, directing and controlling.

Davis includes planning, organizing and controlling. Breach includes planning, organizing, motivating, coordinating and controlling.

Evolution of Management Functions

1. Early concepts	Plan	Organize	Command	Discipline
2. Management Process by Fayol	Plan	Organize	Command coordinate	Control
3. Further modification	Plan	Organize	Direct	Control
4. Modified by behavioural influence	Plan	Organize	Motivate	Control
5. Recent modification by business	Plan	Organize	Integrate	Measure
6. Suggested further	Plan	Organize	Achieve	Appraise

Source : Ervin Williams, "Evaluation of Organic Management Function", Atlanta Economic Review, April 1971, p. 27.

For our purpose, we shall designate the following six as the functions of a manager: planning, organizing, staffing, directing, coordinating and controlling.

Henry Fayol, an early thinker of management process, has classified management functions into planning, organizing, commanding, coordinating and controlling.

Gullick and Urwick have described the functions of management as POSDCORB referring to planning, organizing, staffing, directing, coordinating, reporting and budgeting.

Koontz and O'Donell have included planning, organizing, staffing, leading and controlling.

Earnest Dale has suggested innovation and representing also as important management functions besides these. Thus it can be seen that there is no agreement over the various functions of management. These functions have been treated differently over the period of time.

Ervin Williams has summarized the various managerial functions developed over the period of time.

All the above functions can be categorized into four basic functions of management i.e. planning, organizing, leading and controlling.

3.3.1. Planning

The planning function is the primary activity of management. Planning is the process of establishing goals and a suitable course of action for achieving those goals. Planning implies that managers think through their goals and actions in advance and that their actions are based on some method, plan, or logic rather than on a....... Plans give the organization its objectives and set up the best procedures for reaching them. The organizing, leading and controlling functions all derived from the planning function.

The first step in the planning is the selection of goals for the organization. Goals are then established for each of the organization's subunits-its division, department and soon. Once these are determined, programs are established for achieving goals in a systematic manner.

The organizational objectives are set by top management in the context of its basic purpose and mission, environmental factors, business forecasts, and available and potential resources. These objectives are both long-range as well as short-range. They are divided into divisional, departmental, sectional and individual objectives or goals. This is followed by the development of strategies and courses of action to be followed at various levels of management and in various segments of the organization. Policies, procedures and rules provide the framework of decision making, and the method and order for the making and implementation of these decisions.

Every manager performs all these planning functions, or contributes to their performance. In some organizations, particularly those which are traditionally managed and the small ones, planning are often not done deliberately and systematically but it is still done. The plans may be in the minds of their managers rather than explicitly and precisely spelt out: they may be fuzzy rather than clear but they are always there. Planning is thus the most basic function of management. It is performed in all kinds of organizations by all managers at all levels of hierarchy.

Relationship and time are central to planning activities. Planning produces a picture of desirable future circumstances - given currently available resources, past experience etc. Planning is done by all managers at every level of the organization. Through their plans, managers outline what the organization must do to be successful while plans may differ in focus, they are all concerned with achieving organizational goals in the short and long term. Taken as a whole, an organization's plans are the primary tools for preparing for and dealing with changes in the organization's environment.

3.3.2 Organizing

After managers develop objectives and plans to achieve the objectives, they must design and develop an organization that will be able to accomplish the objectives. Thus the purpose of the organizing function is to create a structure of task and authority relationships that serves this purpose.

Organizing is the process of arranging and allocating work, authority, and resources among an organization's members so they can achieve the organization's goals.

Stoner defines "organizing as the process of engaging two or more people in working together in a structured way to achieve a specific goal or set of goals.

The organizing function takes the tasks identified during planning and assigns them to individuals and groups within the organization so that objectives set by planning can be achieved. Organizing, then, can be thought of turning plans into actions. Organizing function can be viewed as a bridge connecting the conceptual idea developed in creating and planning to the specific means for accomplishing these ideas.

The organizing function also provides on organizational structure that enables the organization to function effectively. Managers must match an organization's structure to its goals and resources, a process called organizational design. Organizing thus involves the following sub-functions:

(a) Identification of activities required for the achievement of objectives and implementation of plans.

(b) Grouping the activities so as to create self-contained jobs.

(c) Assignment of jobs to employees.

(d) Delegation of authority so as to enable them to perform their jobs and to command the resources needed for their performance.

(e) Establishment of a network of coordinating relationships.

Organizing process results in a structure of the organization. It comprises organizational positions, accompanying tasks and responsibilities, and a network of roles and authority-responsibility relationships.

Organizing is thus the basic process of combining and integrating human, physical and financial resources in productive interrelationships for the achievement of enterprise objectives. It aims at combining employees and interrelated tasks in an orderly manner so that organizational work is performed in a coordinated manner, and all efforts and activities pull together in the direction of organizational goals.

3.3.3 Staffing

Staffing is a continuous and vital function of management. After the objectives have been determined, strategies, policies, programmes, procedures and rules formulated for their achievement, activities for the implementation of strategies, policies, programmes, etc. identified and grouped into jobs, the next logical step in the management process is to procure suitable personnel for manning the jobs. Since the efficiency and effectiveness of an organization significantly depends on the quality of its personnel and since it is one of the primary functions of management to achieve qualified and trained people to fill various positions, staffing has been recognized as a distinct function of management. It comprises several sub-functions :

(a) Manpower planning involving determination of the number and the kind of personnel required.

(b) Recruitment for attracting adequate number of potential employees to seek jobs in the enterprise.

(c) Selection of the most suitable persons for the jobs under consideration.

(d) Placement, induction and orientation.

(e) Transfers, promotions, termination and layoff.

(f) Training and development of employees.

As the importance of human factor in organizational effectiveness is being increasingly recognized, staffing is gaining acceptance as a distinct function of management. It need hardly any emphasize that no organization can ever be better than its people, and managers must perform the staffing function with as much concern as any other function.

3.3.4 Directing

Directing is the function of leading the employees to perform efficiently, and contribute their optimum to the achievement of organizational objectives. Jobs assigned to subordinates have to be explained and clarified, they have to be provided guidance in job performance and they are to be motivated to contribute their optimum performance with zeal and enthusiasm. The function of directing thus involves the following sub-functions:

(a) Communication

(b) Motivation

(c) Leadership

Once objectives have been developed and the organizational structure has been designed and staffed, the next step is to begin to move the organization toward the objectives. The directing function serves this purpose. It involves directing, influencing and motivating employees to perform essential tasks.

The best human resources employed will be of house if they are not motivated and directed in the right direction to achieve the organizational goals. Managers lead is an attempt to persuade others to join them in pursuit of the future that emerges from the planning, and organizing steps. By establishing the proper atmosphere, managers help their employees to do their best.

Effective leadership is a highly prized ability in organizations and is a skill that some managers have difficulty in developing. The ability requires both task-oriented capabilities and the ability to communicate, understand and motivate people.

3.3.5 Coordinating

Coordinating is the function of establishing such relationships among various parts of the organization that they all together pull in the direction of organizational objectives. It is thus the process of tying together all the organizational decisions, operations, activities and efforts so as to achieve unity of action for the accomplishment of organizational objectives.

The significance of the coordinating process has been aptly highlighted by Mary Parker Follet. The manager, in her view, should ensure that he has an organization "with all its parts coordinated, so moving together in their closely knit and adjusting activities, so linking, interlocking and interrelation, that they make a working unit that is not a congeries of separate pieces, but what I have called a functional whole or integrative unity". Coordination, as a management function, involves the following sub-functions :

(a) Clear definition of authority-responsibility relationships

(b) Unity of direction

(c) Unity of command

(d) Effective communication

(e) Effective leadership

3.3.6 Controlling

Finally, the manager must be sure that actions of the organizations members do in fact move the organization towards its stated goals. This is the controlling function of management. The controlling is the process of ensuring that actual activities confirm to plan activities. It involves four main elements :-

1. Establishing standards of performance

2. Measuring current performance

3. Comparing this performance to the established standards.

4. Taking correction actions if deviations are detected.

Controlling implies that objectives, goals and standards of performance exist and are known to employees and their superiors. It also implies a flexible and dynamic organization which will permit changes in objectives, plans, programmes, strategies, policies, organizational design, staffing policies and practices, leadership style, communication system, etc., for it is not uncommon that employees failure to achieve predetermined standards is due to defects or shortcomings in any one or more of the above dimensions of management.

Thus, controlling involves the following process :

(a)   Measurement of performance against predetermined goals.

(b)   Identification of deviations from these goals.

(c)   Corrective action to rectify deviations.

It may be pointed out that although management functions have been discussed in a particular sequence-planning, organizing, staffing, directing, coordinating and controlling – they are not performed in a sequential order. Management is an integral process and it is difficult to put its functions neatly in separate boxes. Management functions tend to coalesce, and it sometimes becomes difficult to separate one from the other. For example, when a production manager is discussing work problems with one of his subordinates, it is difficult to say whether he is guiding, developing or communicating, or doing all these things simultaneously. Moreover, managers often perform more than one function simultaneously.

Through the controlling function, managers keep the organization on track. Without the controlling functions, other functions loose their relevance. If all the activities are properly planned, organized and directed but there is no control on the activities then there are full chances that the organization does not achieve its planned goals. Controlling function helps us knowing the deviations but the reasons for such deviations and the corrective actions is to be taken depends on the managers. Hence, the personal ability of the managers makes the controlling function effective or ineffective.

3.4 SUMMARY

In every field of study, first there are basic principles which are practiced later in the forms of certain functions but management is a field where principles are exclusively based on practical experiences. The above named functions of management which have been discussed in this lesson are the backbone of management philosophy. These functions are interrelated as well and we need to perform them in sequenced order for getting the organizational objectives accomplished. But today's environment of business is a perfect blend of all these typical functions. Thus, every function is exercisable according to the situations and perception of managers.

Successful leaders and managers are very energetic. They exert a great deal of effort in order to communicate effectively, solve problems, make decisions, set goals, plan, execute plans, and supervise/ evaluate. These are a leader's directional (or thinking) and implementing skills. As a leader, you cannot expect positive results from your subordinates unless you work equally hard at solving problems, making plans, and putting plans and decisions into action. Successful leaders also work hard at accomplishing their missions and objectives while maintaining only the highest possible standards of performance. Therefore, you being student of management should strive to exercise the same degree of effort and excellence.

3.5 SELF ASSESSMENT QUESTIONS

1. "There is no important area of human activity than management since its task is that of getting things done through people". Discuss the statement and explain with examples.

2. "Management starts from planning and ends up with controlling". Discuss this statement, giving suitable examples.

3. What are the functions of a manager? Is mere knowledge of management enough to become successful manager?

4. Discuss the important functions of management which support the philosophy of modern management thinkers.

3.6 FURTHER READINGS

1. Kootnz & O'Donnell, Principles of Management.
2. Peter F. Drucker, Practice of Management
3. J.S. Chandan, Management Concepts and Strategies.
4. Arun Kumar & Rachana Sharma, Principles of Business Management.

PLANNING

PLANNING

Objectives : The objectives of this lesson are to understand and the nature and process of planning; to appreciate, why it is necessary to do planning; to understand the merits and demerits of planning; to grasp the principles of planning and to understand the various kinds and level of plans.

Lesson Structure:

4.1   The Concept of Planning

4.2   Myths about Planning

4.3   Nature and Scope of Planning

4.4   Importance of Planning

4.5   Advantages and Limits of Planning

4.6   Measures to Overcome Limitations of Planning

4.7   Basic Principles of Planning

4.8   Categories and Levels of Planning

4.9   Essential Steps in Planning

4.10   Summary

4.11   Self Assessment Questions

4.12   Suggested Readings

4.1 THE CONCEPT OF PLANNING

Planning is the most fundamental function of management. An organization can succeed in effective utilization of its human financial and material resources only when its management decides in advance its objectives, and methods of achieving them. Without it purposive and coordinated effort is not possible, and what results are chaos, confusion and wastage of resources. Planning involves determination of objectives of the business, formation of programmes and courses of action for their attainment, development of schedules and timings of action and assignment of responsibilities for their implementation. Planning thus precedes all efforts and action, as it is the plans and programmes that determine the kind of decisions and activities required for the attainment of the desired goals. It lies at the basis of all other managerial functions including organizing, staffing, directing and controlling. In the absence of planning, it will be impossible to decide what activities are required, how they should be combined into jobs and departments, who will be responsible for what kind of decisions and actions, and how various decisions and activities are to be coordinated. And, in the absence of organizing involving the above managerial activities, staffing cannot proceed, and directing cannot be exercised. Planning is also an essential prerequisite for the performance of control function, as it provides criteria for evaluating performance. Planning thus precedes all managerial functions.

Definition of Planning : Planning is the process of deciding in advance what is to be done, who is to do it, how it is to be done and when it is to be done. It is the process of determining a course of action, so as to achieve the desired results. It helps to bridge the gap from where we are, to where we want to go. It makes it possible for things to occur which would not otherwise happen. Planning is a higher order mental process requiring the use of intellectual faculties, imagination, foresight and sound judgment. According to Koontz, O'Donnell and Weihrich, *"Planning is an intellectually demanding process; it requires the conscious determination of courses of action and the basing of decisions on purpose, knowledge and considered estimates"*.

Planning is a process which involves anticipation of future course of events and deciding the best course of action. It is a process of thinking before doing. To plan is to produce a scheme for future action; to bring about specified results, at specified cost, in a specified period of time. It is deliberate attempt to influence, exploit, bring about, and control the nature, direction, extent, speed and effects of change. It may even attempt deliberately to create change, remembering always that change (like decision) in any one sector will in the same way affect other sectors. Planning is a deliberate and conscious effort done to formulate the design and orderly sequence actions through which it is expected to reach the objectives. Planning is a systematic attempt to decide a particular course of action for the future, it leads to determination of objectives of the group activity and the steps necessary to achieve them. Thus, it can be said that planning is the selecting and relating of facts and the making and using of assumptions regarding the future in the visualization and formulation of proposed activities believed necessary to achieve desired results.

Planning is thus deciding in advance the future state of business of an enterprise, and the means of attaining it. Its elements are :

1. What will be done – what are the objectives of business in the short and in the long run?

2. What resources will be required – This involves estimation of the available and potential resources, estimation of resources required for the achievement of objectives, and filling the gap between the two, if any.

3. How it will be done – This involves two things : (i) determination of tasks, activities, projects, programmes, etc., required for the attainment of objectives, and (ii) formulation of strategies, policies, procedures, methods, standard and budgets for the above purpose.

4. Who will do it – It involves assignment of responsibilities to various managers relating to contributions they are expected to make for the attainment of enterprise objectives. This is preceded by the breaking down of the total enterprise objectives into segmental objectives, resulting into divisional, departmental, sectional and individual objectives.

5. When it will be done – It involves determination of the timing and sequence, if any, for the performance of various activities and execution of various projects and their parts.

4.2 MYTHS ABOUT PLANNING

There are certain commonly prevalent myths and fallacies about planning. An attempt is being made to highlight some of the important concepts of planning by way of its distinguishing features, so as to clarify the misconceptions:

(i) **Planning does no attempt to make future decisions :** Planning choosing of the more desirable future alternatives open to a company, is the process so that better decisions may be made.

Planning provides a frame of reference within which the present decisions are to be made. At the same time, a plan often leads to additional but related decisions. For example, a college plan to introduce a new degree or diploma, necessitates the need for decisions like what should be the duration of the course leading to the degree or diploma, together with detailed curricula in the specific courses to be included, the system of evaluation of examination, and the necessary practical training, if any, etc.

(ii) **Planning is not just forecasting or making projections** : Forecasts are mere estimates of the future, and indicate what may or may not happen. However, corporate planning goes beyond these forecasts and asks questions like :

(a) Are we in right business?

(b) What are our basic goals and objectives?

(c) When shall our present products become obsolete?

(d) Are our markets expanding or shrinking?

(e) Do we want to merge or go for takeover?

(iii) **Planning is not a static process** : Indeed, plans are obsolete as soon as they are executed, because the environment assumed in their preparation may have already changed. Planning is a continuous process. It involves continuous analysis and adjustments of the plans and even objectives in the context of changing circumstances.

4.3 NATURE AND SCOPE OF PLANNING

The nature of planning can be understood by focusing on its following aspects :

1. **Planning is a Continuous Process**

Planning deals with the future, and future, by its very nature, is uncertain. Although the planner bases his plans on an informed and intelligent estimate of the future, the future events may not turnout to be exactly as predicted. This aspect of planning makes it a continuous process. Plans tend to be a statement of future intentions relating to objectives and means of their attainment. They do not acquire finality because revisions are needed to be made in them in response to changes taking place in the internal as well as external environment of enterprise. Planning should, therefore, be a continuous process and hence no plan is final, it is always subject to a revision.

2. **Planning concerns all Managers**

It is the responsibility of every manager to set his goals and operating plans. In doing so, he formulates his goals and plans within the framework of the goals and plans of his superior. Thus, planning is not the responsibility of the top management or the staff of planning department only; all those who are responsible for the achievement of results, have an obligation to plan into the future. However, managers at higher levels, being responsible for a relatively larger unit of the enterprise, devote a larger part of their time to planning, and the time span of their plans also tends to be longer than that of managers at lower levels. It shows that planning acquires greater importance and tends to the longer in the future at higher than at lower management levels.

3. **Plans are arranged in a Hierarchy**

Plans are first set for the entire organization called the corporate plan. The corporate plan provides the framework for the formulation of divisional departmental and sectional goals. Each of these organizational components sets its plans laying down the programmes, projects, budgets, resource requirements, etc. The plans of each lower component are aggregated into the plans of successively higher component until the corporate plan integrates all component plans into a composite whole. For example, in the production department, each shop superintendent sets his plans, which are successively integrated into the general foremen's, works manager's and production manager's plans. All departmental plans are then integrated in the corporate plan. Thus, there is a hierarchy of plans comprising the corporate plan, divisional/department plans, sectional plans and individual manger's unit plans.

4. **Planning Commits an Organization into the Future**

   Planning commits an organization into the future, as past, present and future is tied in a chain. An organization's objectives, strategies, policies and operating plans affect its future effectiveness, as decisions made and activities undertaken in the present continue to have their impact into the future. Some of the plans affect the near future, while others affect it in the long run. For example, plans for product diversification or production capacity affect a company long into the future, and are not easily reversible, whereas plans relating to the layout of its office locations can be changed with relatively less difficulty in the future. This focuses on the need for better and more careful planning.

5. **Planning is Antithesis of States Quo**

   Planning is undertaken with the conscious purpose of attaining a position for the company that would not be accomplished otherwise.

Planning, therefore, implies change in organizational objectives, policies, products, marketing strategies and so forth. However, planning itself is affected by unforeseen environmental changes. It, therefore, needs examination and re-examination, continual reconsideration of the future, constant searching for more effective methods and improved results.

Planning is thus an all pervasive, continuous and dynamic process. It imposes on all executives a responsibility to estimate and anticipate the future, prepare the organization to cope with its challenges as well as take advantage of the opportunities created by it, while at the same time, influence tomorrow's events by today's pre-emptive decisions and actions.

4.4 IMPORTANCE OF PLANNING

While planning does not guarantee success in organizational objectives, there is evidence that companies that engaged in formal planning consistently performed better than those with none or limited formal planning and improved their own performance over a period of time. It is very rare for an organization to succeed solely by luck or circumstances. Some of the reasons as to why planning is considered a vital managerial function are given below :

1. **Planning is essential in modern business :** The growing complexity of the modern business with rapid technological changes, dynamic changes in the consumer preferences and growing tough competition necessities orderly operations, not only in the current environment but also in the future

environment. Since planning takes a future outlook, it takes into account the possible future developments.

2. **Planning affects performance :** A number of empirical studies provide evidence of organizational success being a function of formal planning, the success being measured by such factors as return on investment, sales volume, growth in earnings per share and so on. An investigation of firms in various industrial products as machinery, steel, oil, chemicals and drugs revealed that companies that engaged in formal planning consistently performed better than those with no formal planning.

3. **Planning puts focus on objectives :** The effectiveness of formal planning is primarily based upon clarity of objectives. Objectives provide a direction and all planning decisions are directed towards achievement of these objectives. Plans continuously reinforce the importance of these objectives by focusing on them. This ensures maximum utility of managerial time and efforts.

4. **Planning anticipates problems and uncertainties :** A significant aspect of any formal planning process in collection of relevant information for the purpose of forecasting the future as accurately as possible. This would minimize the chances of haphazard decisions. Since the future needs of the organization are anticipated in advance, the proper acquisition and allocation of resources can be planned, thus minimizing wastage and ensuring optimal utility of these resources.

5. **Planning is necessary to facilitate control :** Controlling involves the continual analysis and measurement of actual operations against the established standards. These standards are set in the light of objectives to by achieved. Periodic reviews of operations can determine whether the plans are being implemented correctly. Well developed plans can aid the process of control in two ways.

    First, the planning process establishes a system of advance warning of possible deviations from the expected performance. Second contribution of planning to the control process is that it provides quantitative data which would make it easier to compare the actual performance in quantitative terms, not only with the expectations of the organization but also with the industry statistics or market forecasts.

6. **Planning helps in the process of decision making :** Since planning specifies the actions and steps to be taken in order to accomplish organizational objectives, it serves as a basis for decision-making about future activities. It also helps managers to make routine decisions about current activities since the objectives, plans, policies, schedules and so on are clearly laid down.

4.5 ADVANTAGES AND LIMITATIONS OF PLANNING

The importance of formal planning has already been discussed. A vigorous and detailed planning programme helps managers to be future oriented. It gives the mangers some purpose and direction. A sound blue print for plans with specific objective and action statements has numerous advantages for the organization which are as follows :

1. **Focuses Attention on Objectives :** Since all planning is directed towards achieving enterprise objectives, the very act of planning focuses attention on these objectives. Laying down the objectives is the first step in planning. If the objectives are clearly laid down, the execution of plans will also be directed towards these objectives.

2. **Ensures Economical Operation :** Planning involves a lot of mental exercise which is directed towards achieving efficient operation in the enterprise. It substitutes joint directed effort for uncoordinated piecemeal activity, even flow of work for uneven flow, and deliberate decisions for snap judgement costs. This helps in better utilization of resources and thus minimizing costs.

3. **Reduces Uncertainty :** Planning helps in reducing uncertainties of future because it involves anticipation of future events. Effective planning is the result of deliberate thinking based on facts and figures. It involves forecasting also. Planning gives an opportunity to a business manager to foresee various uncertainties which may be caused by changes in technology, taste and fashion of the people, etc. Sufficient provision is made in the plans to offset these uncertainties.

4. **Facilitates Control :** Planning helps the managers in performing their function of control. Planning and control are inseparable in the sense that unplanned action cannot be controlled because control involves keeping activities on the predetermined course by rectifying deviations from plans. Planning helps control by furnishing standards of control. It lays down objectives and standards of

performance which are essential for the performance of control function.

5. **Encourages Innovation and Creativity :** Planning is basically the deciding function of management. It helps innovative and creative thinking among the managers because many new ideas come to the mind of a manager when he is planning. It creates a forward looking attitude among the managers.

6. **Improves Motivation :** A good planning system ensures participation of all managers which improves their motivation. It improves the motivation of workers also because they know clearly what is expected of them. Moreover, planning serves as a good training device for future managers.

7. **Improves Competitive Strength :** Effective planning gives a competitive edge to the enterprise over other enterprises that do not have planning or have ineffective planning. This is because planning may involve expansion of capacity, changes in work methods, changes in quality, anticipation tastes and fashion of people and technological changes, etc.

8. **Achieves Better Coordination :** Planning secures unity of direction towards the organizational objectives. All the activities are directed towards the common goals. There is an integrated effort throughout the enterprise. It will also help in avoiding duplication of efforts. Thus, there will be better coordination in the organization.

Limitations of Planning : Sometimes, planning fails to achieve the expected results. There are many causes of failure of planning in practice. These are discussed below :

1. **Lack of reliable data :** There may be lack of reliable facts and figures over which plans may be based. Planning loses its value if reliable information is not available or if the planner fails to utilize the reliable information. In order to make planning successful, the planner must determine the reliability of facts and figures and must base his plans on reliable information only.

2. **Lack of initiative :** Planning is a forward looking process. If a manager has a tendency to follow rather than lead, he will not be able to make good plans. Therefore, the planner must take the required initiative. He should be an active planner and should take adequate follow up measure to see that plans are understood and implemented properly.

3. **Costly process :** Planning is time consuming and expensive process. This may delay action in certain cases. But it is also true that if sufficient time is not given to the planning process, the plans so produced may prove to be unrealistic. Similarly, planning involves costs of gathering and analyzing information and evaluation of various alternatives. If the management is not willing to spend on planning, the results may not be good.

4. **Rigidity in organizational working :** Internal inflexibility in the organization may compel the planners to make rigid plans. This may deter the managers from taking initiative and doing innovative thinking. So the planners must have sufficient discretion and flexibility in the enterprise. They should not always be required to follow the procedures rigidly.

5. **Non-acceptability of change :** Resistance to change is another factor which puts limits on planning. It is a commonly experienced

phenomenon in the business world. Sometimes, planners themselves do not like change and on other occasions they do not think it desirable to bring change as it makes the planning process ineffective.

6. **External limitations :** The effectiveness of planning is sometimes limited because of external factors which are beyond the control of the planners. External strategies are very difficult to predict. Sudden break-out of war, government control, natural havocs and many other factors are beyond the control of management. This makes the execution of plans very difficult.

7. **Psychological barriers :** Psychological factors also limit the scope of planning. Some people consider present more important than future because present is certain. Such persons are psychologically opposed to planning. But it should not be forgotten that dynamic mangers always look ahead. Long-range wellbeing of the enterprise cannot be achieved unless proper planning is done for future.

4.6 MEASURES TO OVERCOME LIMITATIONS OF PLANNING

Some people say that planning is a mere ritual in the fast changing environment. This is not a correct assessment on managerial planning. Planning may be associated with certain difficulties such as non-availability of data, lethargy on the part of the planners, rigidity of procedures, resistance to change and changes in external environment. But these problems can be overcome by taking the following steps :

1. **Setting Clear-cut Objectives :** The existence of clear-cut objectives is necessary for efficient planning. Objectives should not only be understandable but rational also. The overall objectives of the

enterprise must be the guiding pillars for determining the objectives of various departments. This would help in having coordinated planning in the enterprise.

2. **Management Information System :** An efficient system of management information should be installed so that all relevant facts and figures are made available to the mangers before they perform the planning function. Availability of right type of information will help in overcoming the problems of complete understanding of the objectives and resistance to change on the part of the subordinates.

3. **Carefully Premising :** The planning premises constitute a framework within which planning is done. They are the assumptions of what is likely to happen in future. Planning always requires some assumptions to be made regarding future happenings. In other words, it is a prerequisite to determine future settings such as marketing, pricing, Government policy, tax structure, business cycle, etc. before giving the final shape to the overall business plan. Due weightage should be given to the relevant factors at the time of premising. It may be pointed out that the premises which may be of strategic significance to one enterprise may not be of equal significance to another because of size, nature of business, nature of market, etc.

4. **Business Forecasting :** Business is greatly influenced by economic, social, political and international environment. The management must have a mechanism of forecasting changes in such environment. Good forecasts will contribute to the effectiveness of planning.

5. **Dynamic Managers :** The persons concerned with the task of planning should be dynamic in outlook. They must take the required initiative to make business forecasts and develop planning premises.

A manager should always keep in mind that planning is looking ahead and he is making plans for future which is highly uncertain.

6. **Flexibility :** Some element of flexibility must be introduced in the planning process because modern business operates in an environment which keeps on changing. For achieving effective results, there should always be a scope to make necessary addition, deletion, or alternation in the plans as is demanded by the circumstances.

7. **Availability of Resources :** Determination and evaluation of alternatives should be done in the light of resources available to the management. Alternatives are always present in any decision problem. But their relative plus and minus points are to be evaluated in the light of the resources available. The alternative which is chosen should not only be concerned with the objectives of the enterprise, but also capable of being accomplished with the help of the given resources.

8. **Cost-Benefit Analysis :** The planners must undertake cost-benefit analysis to ensure that the benefits of planning are more than the cost involved in it. This necessarily calls for establishing measurable goals, clear insight to the alternative courses of action available, premising reasonable and formulation of derivative plans keeping in view the fact that environment is fast changing.

4.7 BASIC PRINCIPLES OF PLANNING

The important principles of planning are as follows:

1. **Principle of contribution to objective :** The purpose of plans and their components is to develop and facilitate the realization of organizational aims and objectives. Long-range plans should be interwoven with medium-range plans which, in turn, should be meshed with short-range ones in order to accomplish organizational objectives more effectively and economically.

2. **Principle of limiting factors :** Planning must take the limiting factors (manpower, money, machines, materials, and management) into account by concentrating on them when developing alternative plans, strategies, policies, procedures and standards.

3. **Principle of pervasiveness of planning :** Planning is found at all levels of management. Strategic planning or long-range planning is related to top management, while intermediate and short-range planning is the concern of middle and operative management respectively.

4. **Principle of navigational change :** This principle requires that managers should periodically check on events and redraw plans to maintain a course towards a desired goal. It is the duty of the navigator to check constantly, whether his ship is following the right direction in the vast ocean to reach the distinction as scheduled. In the same way, a manager should check his plans to ensure that these are processing as required. He should change the direction of his plans if he faces unexpected events. It is useful if plans contain an element of flexibility. It is the responsibility of the manager, to adapt and change the direction of plans, to meet the challenge of constantly changing environment that could not be foreseen.

5. **Principle of flexibility :** Flexibility should be built into organizational plans. Possibility of error in forecasting and decision-making and future uncertainties is the two common factors which call for flexibility in managerial planning. The principal of flexibility states the management should be able to change an existing plan because of changes in environment, without due cost or delay, so that activities keep moving towards established goals. Thus, an unexpected slump in demand for a product will require change in sales plan as well ass production plan. Change in these plans can be introduced, only when these possess the characteristics of flexibility. Adapting plans to suit future uncertainties or changing environment is easier if flexibility is an important consideration while planning.

4.8 CATEGORIES AND LEVELS OF PLANNING

Planning can be classified on different bases which are discussed below :

1. **Strategic and Functional Planning :** In strategic or corporate planning, the top management determines the general objectives of the enterprise and the steps necessary to accomplish them in the light of resources currently available and likely to be available in the future. Functional planning, on the other hand, is planning that covers functional areas like production, marketing, finance and purchasing.

2. **Long-range and short-range planning :** Long-range planning sets long-term goals of the enterprise and then proceeds to formulate specific plans for attaining these goals. It involves an attempt to anticipate, analyze and make decisions about basic problems and issues which have significance reaching well beyond the present

operating horizon of the enterprise. Short-range planning, on the other hand, is concerned with the determination of short-term activities to accomplish long-term with the determination of short-term activities to accomplish long-term objectives. Short range planning relates to a relatively short period and has to be consistent with the long-range plans. Operational plans are generally related to short periods.

3. **Adhoc and Standing Planning :** Adhoc planning committees may be constituted for certain specific matters, as for instance, for project planning. But standing plans are designed to be used over and over again. They include organizational structure, standard procedures, standard methods etc.

4. **Administrative and Operational Planning :** Administrative planning is done by the middle level management which provides the foundation for operative plans. Operative planning, on the other hand, is done by the lower level mangers to put the administrative plans into action.

5. **Physical Planning :** It is concerned with the physical location and arrangement of building and equipment.

6. **Formal and Informal Planning :** Various types of planning discussed above are of formal nature. They are carried on systematically by the management. They specify in black and white the specific goals and the steps to achieve them. They also facilitate the installation of internal control systems. Informal planning, on the other hand, is mere thinking by some individuals which may become the basis of formal planning in future.

LEVELS OF PLANNING

In management theory it is usual to consider that there are three basic level of planning, though in practice there may be more than three levels of management and to an extent there will be some overlapping of planning operations. The three level of planning are as under :

1. **Top Level Planning :** Also known as overall or strategic planning, top level planning is done by the top management, i.e. board of directors or governing body. It encompasses the long-range objectives and policies of organization and is concerned with corporate results rather than sectional objective. Top level planning is entirely long-range and is inextricably linked with long-term objectives. It might be called the 'what' of planning.

2. **Second Level Planning :** Also known as tactical planning, it is done by middle level mangers or department heads. It is concerned with 'how' of planning. It deals with deployment of resources to the best advantage. It is concerned mainly, but not exclusively, with long-range planning, but its nature is such that the time spans are usually shorter than those of strategic planning. This is because its attentions are usually devoted to the step by step attainment of the organization's main objectives. It is, in fact, oriented to functions and departments rather than to the organization as a whole.

3. **Third Level Planning :** Also known as operational or activity planning, it is the concern of department managers and supervisors. It is confined to putting into effect the tactical or departmental plans. It is usually for short-term and may be revised quite often to be in tune with the tactical planning.

4.9 ESSENTIAL STEPS IN PLANNING

Planning is a process which embraces a number of steps to be taken. It is an intellectual exercise and a conscious determination of courses of action. Therefore, it requires a serious thought on numerous factors necessary to be considered in making plans. Facts are collected and analyzed and the best out of all is chosen and adopted. The planning process, valid for one organization and for one plan, may not be valid for all other organizations or all types of plans, because various factors that go into planning process may differ from organization to organization or plan to plan. For example, planning process for a large organization may not be the same as for a small organization. The steps generally involved in planning are as follows :

1. **Establishing Verifiable Goals or Set of Goals to be Achieved :** The first step in planning is to determine the enterprise objectives. These are most often set by upper level or top managers, usually after a number of possible objectives have been carefully considered. There are many types of objectives managers may select: a desired sales volume or growth rate, the development of a new product or service, or even a more abstract goal such as becoming more active in the community. The type of goal selected will depend on number of factors: the basic mission of the organization, the values its managers hold, and the actual and potential ability of the organization.

2. **Establishing Planning Premises :** The second step in planning is to establish planning premises, i.e. certain assumptions about the future on the basis of which the plan will be intimately formulated. Planning premises are vital to the success of planning as

they supply economic conditions, production costs and prices, probable competitive behaviour, capital and material availability, governmental control and so on.

3. **Deciding the planning period :** Once upper-level managers have selected the basic long-term goals and the planning premises, the next task is to decide the period of the plan. Business varies considerably in their planning periods. In some instances plans are made for a year only while in others they span decades. In each case, however, there is always some logic in selecting a particular time range for planning. Companies generally base their period on a future that can reasonably be anticipated. Other factors which influence the choice of a period are as follows: : (a) lead time in development and commercialization of a new product; (b) time required to recover capital investments or the pay back period; and (c) length of commitments already made.

4. **Findings Alternative Courses of Action :** The fourth step is planning is to search for and examining alternative courses of action. For instance, technical know-how may be secured by engaging a foreign technician or by training staff abroad. Similarly, products may be sold directly to the consumer by the company's salesmen or through exclusive agencies. There is seldom a plan for which reasonable alternatives do not exit, and quite often an alternative that is not obvious proves to be the best.

5. **Evaluating and Selecting a Course of Action :** Having sought alternative courses, the fifth step is to evaluate them in the light of the premises and goals and to select the best course or courses of action. This is done with the help of quantitative techniques and operations research.

6. **Developing Derivative plans :** Once the plan has been formulated, its broad goals must be translated into day-to-day operations of the organization. Middle and lower-level managers must draw up the appropriate plans, programmes and budgets for their sub-units. These are described as derivative plans. In developing these derivative plans, lower-level managers take steps similar to those taken by upper-level managers – selecting realistic goals, assessing their sub-units particular strength and weaknesses and analyzing those parts of the environment that can affect them.

7. **Measuring and Controlling the Progress :** Obviously, it is foolish to let a plan run its course without monitoring its progress. Hence the process of controlling is a critical part of any plan. Managers need to check the progress of their plans so that they can (a) take whatever remedial action is necessary to make the plan work, or (b) change the original plan if it is unrealistic.

2.10 SUMMARY

Planning has a primacy over other management functions and is a pervasive element in organizations. It involves the major activities such as setting objectives, determining policies and making decisions. Planning is a higher order mental process requiring the use of intellectual faculties, imagination, foresight and sound judgement. By planning managers minimize uncertainty and help focus the sight of their organization on its goals.

2.11 SELF ASSESSMENT QUESTIONS :

1. "Managerial planning seeks to achieve a coordinated structure of operations". Comment.

2. "Without planning an enterprise would soon disintegrate, its actions would be as random as leaves scampering before an autumn wind, and its employee as confused as ants in an upturned ant hill". Comment

3. What do you understand by planning? Define its objectives and assess its importance. What should be done to overcome its limitations?

4. "Planning involves a choice between alternative courses of action". Comment briefly.

5. Describe in detail the steps involved in the planning process.

2.12 SUGGESTED READINGS

1. Kootnz & O'Donnell, Principles of Management.

2. J.S. Chandan, Management Concepts and Strategies.

6. Arun Kumar and R. Sharma, Principles of Business Management.

7. Sherlerkar and Sherlerkar, Principles of Management

8. B.P. Singh, Business Management and Organizations

DECISION MAKING

DEISION-MAKING

Objective : The learning objectives of the lesson are to know the meaning and importance of Decision Making; to understand the characteristics and process of Decision Making; to understand the various types of Decisions and to learn the Techniques of Decision Making.

Lesson Structure:

5.1   The Concept of Decision Making

5.2   Characteristics of Decision Making

5.3   Importance of Decision Making

5.4   Decision Making Process

5.5   Types of Decisions

5.6   Techniques of Decision Making

5.7   Summary

5.8   Self Assessment Questions

5.9   Suggested Readings

5.1 THE CONCEPT OF DECISION MAKING

Decision-making and problem-solving are basic ingredients of managerial leadership. More than anything else, the ability to make sound, timely decisions separates a successful manager from a non-successful. It is the responsibility of managers to make high quality decisions that are accepted and executed in a timely fashion. On the face of it the decisions should be cohesive, conjectured, contingent, flexible, improved, influencing, intuitional, non-judgemental, objective, operational one. One of the most important functions of a manager is to take decisions. Whatever a manager does, he does through decision-making. Each managerial decision is concerned with the process of decision-making. It is because of this pervasiveness of decision-making that Professor Herbert Simon has said the process of managing as a process of decision-making. According to him, a post or position cannot be said to be managerial level until and unless the right of decision-making is attached to it. As a matter of act, it is the core of executive activities in a business organization.

Decision-making is a mental process. It is a process of selecting one best alternative for doing a work. Thus, it is a particular course of action chosen by a decision maker as the most effective alternative for achieving his goals. According to D.E. McFarland, "A decision is an act of choice- wherein an executive forms a conclusion about what must be done in a given situation. A decision represents a course of behaviour chosen from a number of possible alternatives". In the words of Haynes and Massie, "A decision is a course of action which is consciously chosen for achieving a desired result".

Hence decision-making is a typical form of planning. It involves choosing the best alternative among various alternatives, in order to realize certain objectives. A decision represents a judgement, a final word, and resolution of conflicts or a commitment to act in certain manner in the given set of circumstances. It is really a mental exercise which decides what to do.

Leaders must be able to reason under the most critical conditions and decide quickly what action to take. If they delay or avoid making a decision, this indecisiveness may create hesitancy, loss of confidence, and confusion within the unit, and may cause the task to fail. Since leaders are frequently faced with unexpected circumstances, it is important to be flexible - leaders must be able to react promptly to each situation. Then, when circumstances dictate a change in plans, prompt reaction builds confidence in them.

5.2 CHARACTERISTICS OF DECISION MAKING

The essential characteristics of decision making are given below:

1. It is a process of choosing a course of action from among the alternative courses of action.

2. It is a human process involving to a great extent the application of intellectual abilities.

3. It is the end process preceded by deliberation and reasoning.

4. It is always related to the environment. A manager may take one decision in a particular set of circumstances and another in a different set of circumstances.

5. It involves a time dimension and a time lag.

6. It always has a purpose. Keeping this in view, there may just be a decision not to decide.

7. It involves all actions like defining the problem and probing and analyzing the various alternatives which take place before a final choice is made.

5.3 IMPORTANCE OF DECISION MAKING

As a leader, you will make decisions involving not only yourself, but the morale and welfare of others. Some decisions, such as when to take a break or where to hold a meeting, are simple decisions which have little effect on others. Other decisions are often more complex and may have a significant impact on many people. Therefore, having a decision-making, problem-solving process can be a helpful tool. Such a process can help you to solve these different types of situations. Within business and the military today, leaders at all levels use some form of a decision-making, problem-solving process. There are several different approaches (or models) for decision-making and problem solving. We would briefly discuss it in this lesson as well.

It is beyond doubt that the decision making is an essential part of every function of management. According to Peter F. Drucker, "Whatever a manager does, he does through decision making". Decision making lies deeply embedded in the process of management, spreads over all the managerial functions and covers all the areas of the organization. Management and decision making are bound up and go side by side in every activity performed by manager. Whether knowingly or unknowingly, every manager makes decisions constantly.

Right from the day when the size of the organization used to be very small to the present day huge or mega size of the organization, the importance of decision making has been there. The significant difference is that in today's complex organization structure, the decision making is getting more and more complex. Whatever a manager does, he does through making decisions. Some of the decisions are of routine and repetitive in nature and it might be that the manager does not realize that he is taking decisions whereas, other decisions which are of strategic nature may require a lot of systematic and scientific analysis. The fact remains that management is always a decision making process.

The most outstanding quality of successful manager is his/her ability to make sound and effective decisions. A manager has to make up his/her mind quickly on certain matters. It is not correct to say that he has to make spur of the moment decisions all the time. For taking many decisions, he gets enough time for careful fact finding, analysis of alternatives and choice of the best alternative. Decision making is a human process. When one decides, he chooses a course alternative which he thinks is the best.

Decision making is a proper blend of thinking, deciding and action. An important executive decision is only one event in the process which requires a succession of activities and routine decisions all along the way. Decisions also have a time dimension and a time lag. A manager takes time to collect facts and to weigh various alternatives. Moreover, after decides, it takes still more time to carry out a decision and, often, it takes longer before he can judge whether the decision was good or bad. It is also very difficult to isolate the effects of any single decision.

5.4 DECISION MAKING PROCESS

The following procedure should be followed in arriving at a correct decision:

1. **Setting objectives** : Rational decision-making involves concrete objectives. So the first step in decision-making is to know one's objectives. An objective is an expected outcome of future actions. So

before deciding upon the future course of efforts, it is necessary to know beforehand what we are trying to achieve. Exact knowledge of goals and objectives bring purpose in planning and harmony in efforts. Moreover, objectives are the criteria by which final outcome is to be measured.

2. **Defining the Problem :** It is true to a large extent that a problem well defined is half solved. A lot of bad decisions are made because the person making the decision does not have a good grasp of the problem. It is essential for the decision maker to find and define the problem before he takes any decision.

Sufficient time and energy should be spent on defining the problem as it is not always easy to define the problem and to see the fundamental thing that is causing the trouble and that needs correction. Practically, no problem ever presents itself in a manner that an immediate decision may be taken. It is, therefore, essential to define the problem before any action is taken, otherwise the manager will answer the wrong question rather than the core problem. Clear definition of the problem is very important as the right answer can be found only to a right question.

3. **Analyzing the problem :** After defining the problem, the next step in decision-making is analyzing it. The problem should be thoroughly analyzed to find out adequate background information and data relating to the situation. The problem should be divided into many sub-problems and each element of the problem must be investigated thoroughly and systematically. There can be a number of factors involved with any problem, some of which are pertinent and others are remote. These pertinent factors should be discussed in depth. It will save time as well as money and efforts.

    In order to classify any problem, we require lot of information. So long as the required information is not available, any classification would be misleading. This will also have an adverse impact on the quality of the decision. Trying to analyze without facts is like guessing directions at a crossing without reading the highway signboards. Thus, collection of right type of information is very important in decision making. It would not be an exaggeration to say that a decision is as good as the information on which it is based. Collection of facts and figures also requires certain decisions on the part of the manager. He must decide what type of information he requires and how he can obtain this.

4. **Developing Alternatives :** After defining and analyzing the problem, the next step in the decision making process is the development of alternative courses of action. Without resorting to the process of developing alternatives, a manager is likely to be guided by his limited imagination. It is rare for alternatives to be

lacking for any course of action. But sometimes a manager assumes that there is only one way of doing a thing. In such a case, what the manager has probably not done is to force himself consider other alternatives. Unless he does so, he cannot reach the decision which is the best possible. From this can be derived a key planning principle which may be termed as the principle of alternatives. Alternatives exist for every decision problem. Effective planning involves a search for the alternatives towards the desired goal.

Once the manager starts developing alternatives, various assumptions come to his mind, which he can bring to the conscious level. Nevertheless, development of alternatives cannot provide a person with the imagination, which he lacks. But most of us have definitely more imagination than we generally use. It should also be noted that development of alternatives is no guarantee of finding the best possible decision, but it certainly helps in weighing one alternative against others and, thus, minimizing uncertainties.

While developing alternatives, the principle of limiting factor has to be taken care of. A limiting factor is one which stands in the way of accomplishing the desired goal. It is a key factor in decision making. If such factors are properly identified, manager can confine his search for alternative to those which will overcome the limiting factors. In choosing from among alternatives, the more an individual can recognize those factors which are limiting or critical to the attainment of the desired goal the more clearly and accurately he or she can select the most favourable alternatives.

5. **Selecting the Best Alternative :** After developing alternatives one will have to evaluate all the possible alternatives in order to select best alternative. There are various ways to evaluate alternatives. The

most common method is through intuition, i.e., choosing a solution that seems to be good at that time. There is an inherent danger in this process because a manager's intuition may be wrong on several occasions.

The second way to choose the best alternative is to weigh the consequences of one against those of the others. Peter F. Drucker has laid down four criteria in order to weigh the consequences of various alternatives. They are :

(a) **Risk :** A manager should weigh the risks of each course of action against the expected gains. As a matter of fact, risks are involved in all the solutions. What matters is the intensity of different types of risks in various solutions.

(b) **Economy of Effort :** The best manager is one who can mobilize the resources for the achievement of results with the minimum of efforts. The decision to be chosen should ensure the maximum possible economy of efforts, money and time.

(c) **Situation or Timing :** The choice of a course of an action will depend upon the situation prevailing at a particular point of time. If the situation has great urgency, the preferable course of action is one that alarms the organization that something important is happening. If a long and consistent effort is needed, a slow start gathers momentum approach may be preferable.

(d) **Limitation of Resources :** In choosing among the alternatives, primary attention must be given to those factors that are limiting or strategic to the decision involved. The search for limiting factors in decision-making should be a never ending process. Discovery of the limiting factor lies at the basis of selection from the alternatives and hence of planning and decision making. There are three bases which should be followed for selection of alternatives and these are experience, experimentation and research and analysis which are discussed below :

In making a choice, a manager is influenced to a great extent by his past experience. He can give more reliance to past experience in case of routine decisions; but in case of strategic decisions, he should not rely fully on his past experience to reach at a rational decision.

Under experimentation, the manager tests the solution under actual or simulated conditions. This approach has proved to be of considerable help in many cases in test marketing of a new product. But it is not always possible to put this technique into practice, because it is very expensive.

Research and Analysis is considered to be the most effective technique of selecting among alternatives, where a major decision is involved. It involves a search for relationships among the more critical variables, constraints and premises that bear upon the goal sought.

6. **Implementing the Decision :** The choice of an alternative will not serve any purpose if it is not put into practice. The manager is not only concerned with taking a decision, but also with its implementation. He should try to ensure that systematic steps are taken to implement the decision. The main problem which the manager may face at the implementation stage is the resistance by

the subordinates who are affected by the decision. If the manager is unable to overcome this resistance, the energy and efforts consumed in decision making will go waste. In order to make the decision acceptable, it is necessary for the manager to make the people understand what the decision involves, what is expected to them and what they should expect from the management.

In order to make the subordinates committed to the decision it is essential that they should be allowed to participate in the decision making process. The managers who discuss problems with their subordinates and give them opportunities to ask questions and make suggestions find more support for their decisions than the managers who don't let the subordinates participate. The area where the subordinates should participate is the development of alternatives. They should be encouraged to suggest alternatives. This may bring to surface certain alternatives which may not be thought of by the manager. Moreover, they will feel attached to the decision. At the same time, there is also a danger that a group decision may be poorer than the one man decision. Group participation does not necessarily improve the quality of the decision, but sometimes impairs it. Someone has described group decision like a train in which every passenger has a brake. It has also been pointed out that all employees are unable to participate in decision making. Nevertheless, it is desirable if a manager consults his subordinates while making decision.

7. **Follow-up the Decisions :** Kennetth H. Killer, has emphatically written in his book that it is always better to check the results after putting the decision into practice. He has given reasons for following up of decisions and they are as follows:

(i) If the decision is a good one, one will know what to do if faced with the same problem again.

(ii) If the decision is a bad one, one will know what not to do the next time.

(iii) If the decision is bad and one follows-up soon enough, corrective action may still be possible.

In order to achieve proper follow-up, the management should devise an efficient system of feedback information. This information will be very useful in taking the corrective measures and in taking right decisions in the future.

5.5 TYPES OF DECISIONS

Decisions have been classified by various authorities in various ways. The main types of decisions are as follows :

1. **Programmed and non-programmed decisions :** Professor Herbert Simon has classified all managerial decisions as programmed and non-programmed decisions. He has utilized computer terminology in classifying decisions. The programmed decisions are the routine and repetitive decisions for which the organization has developed specific processes. Thus, they involve no extraordinary judgement, analysis and authority. They are basically devised so that the problem may not be treated as a unique case each time it arises.

On the other hand, the non-programmed decisions are the one-shot, ill structured, novel policy decisions that are handled by general problem-solving processes. Thus, they are of extraordinary nature and require a thorough study of the problem, its in-depth analysis and the solving the problem. They are basically non-repetitive in nature and may be called as strategic decisions.

2. **Basic and routine decisions :** Professor George Katona has made a distinction between basic decision and routine decisions. Routine decisions are of repetitive nature and they involve the application of familiar principles to a situation. Basic or genuine decisions are those which require a good deal of deliberation on new principles through conscious thought process, plant location, distribution are some examples of basic decisions.

3. **Policy and operative decisions :** Policy decisions are important decisions and they involve a change in the procedure, planning or strategy of the organization. Thus, they are of a fundamental character affecting the whole business. Such decisions are taken by the top management. On the contrary, operating decisions are those which are taken by lower levels of management for the purpose of executing policy decisions. They are generally concerned with the routine type of work, hence unimportant for the top management. They mostly relate to the decision-makers own work and behaviour while policy decision influences the work and behaviour of subordinates.

4. **Individual and group decisions :** Individual decisions are those decisions which are made by one individual – whether owner of the business or by a top executive. On the other hand, group-decisions are the decisions taken by a group of managers – board, team, committee or a sub-committee. In India, individual decision-making is still very common because a large number of businesses are small and owned by a single individual. But in joint stock Company's group decisions are common. There are both merits and demerits of each type of decision.

5.6 TOOLS OR TECHNIQUES OF DECISION MAKING

The following are some of the important decision making techniques :

(A) Qualitative Techniques

(B) Quantitative Techniques

(A) Qualitative Decision Making Techniques

There is a great importance of generating a reasonable number of alternatives, so that one can decide upon the better quality items and make better decision.

Generating a reasonable number of alternatives is very useful for solving any complex problem. There are following means of generating the alternatives :

(a) Brainstorming

(b) Synectics, and

(c) Nominal Grouping

(a) Brainstorming

This technique was developed by Alex F. Osborn, and is one of the oldest and best known techniques for stimulating the creative thinking. This is carried out in a group where members are presented with a problem and are asked to develop as many as potential solutions as possible. The member of the group may be experts, may be from other organizations but the members should be around six to eight. The duration of the session may be around 30 minutes to 55 minutes. The premise of brainstorming is that when people interact in a free and exhibited atmosphere, they will generate creative ideas. The idea generated by one person acts as a stimulus for generating idea by others. This generation of ideas is a contagious and creates an atmosphere of free discussion and spontaneous thinking. The major objective of this exercise is to produce as many deals as possible, so that there is greater likelihood of identifying a best solution.

The important rules of brainstorming are as given below :

(i) Criticism is prohibited.

(ii) Freewheeling is always welcome.

(iii) Quantity is desirable.

(iv) Combination and improvements are sought.

One session of brainstorming exercise generates around 50 to 150 ideas. Brainstorming is very useful in research, advertising, management, armed forces, governmental and non-governmental agencies.

Limitations of Brainstorming

The limitations of brainstorming are given below :

(i) It is not very effective when a problem is very complex and vague

(ii) It is time consuming

(iii) It is very costly

(iv) It produces superficial solutions.

(b) Synectics

This technique was developed by William J.J. Gordon. It is recently formalized tool of creative thinking. The word Synectics is a Greek word, meaning the fitting together of diverse elements. The basic purpose of synectics is to stimulate novel and even bizarre alternatives through the joining together of distinct and apparently irrelevant ideas.

The selection of members to synectics group is based on their background and training. The experienced leader states the problem for the group to consider, group reacts to the problem stated on the basis of their understanding and convictions. When the nature of the problem is thoroughly reviewed and analyzed, group proceeds to offer potential solutions. The leader has to structure the problem and he/she can use various methods to involve the preconscious mind, like role-playing, use of analogies, paradoxes, metaphors and other thought provoking exercises. This helps in generation of alternatives. The technical expert assists the group in evaluating the feasibility of ideas. It also suffers from some limitations of brainstorming. This is more useful and appropriate for solving complex and technical problems.

(c) Nominal Grouping : This was developed by Andre Dellbecq and Andrew Van de Ven. Nominal group is very effective in situations where a high degree of innovation and idea generation is required. It is highly structured and follows following stages :

Stage-I : Around seven to ten participants with different background and training are selected, familiarized with a selected problem like what alternatives are available for achieving a set of objective.

Stage-2 : Each member is asked to prepare a list of ideas in response to the identified problem, individually for achieving a set of objective.

Stage -3 : After ten minutes, the member shares ideas, one at a time, in a round-robin manner. The group facilitator records the ideas on a blackboard or flip chart for all to see.

Stage-4: Each group member then openly discusses and evaluates each recorded ideas. At this point, it may be rewarded, combined, added or deleted.

Stage-5: Each member votes ranking the ideas privately. Following a brief discussion of the vote, a final secret ballot is conducted. The group's preference is the arithmetical outcome of the individual voter, these are followed by concluding meeting.

(B) Quantitative Techniques

There are a number of quantitative techniques for decision-making that are discussed below:

(a) **Stochastic Methods**: In many management decisions, the probability of the occurrence of an event can be assumed to be known, even when a particular outcome is unpredictable. Under these conditions of risk, stochastic methods will be useful. Actually, stochastic methods merely systematize the thinking about assumptions, facts and goals that is involved in decisions under conditions of risk.

Three steps are basic to formalizing the factors to be considered in a decision involving probabilities: (i) The decision maker should first lay out, in tabular form, all the possible actions that seem reasonable to consider and all the possible outcomes of these actions (ii) The decision maker must then state in quantitative form a probability distribution, projecting chances of each outcome that might result from each act. In this step, it may only be possible to assign probabilities that are reasonable estimates. The key to this step is to state explicitly the various probabilities that might be attached to each act-outcome situation (iii) finally, the decision maker must use some quantitative yardstick of value (usually rupees) that measures the value of each outcome. It is then possible to calculate an average of the outcome-values weighted by the assigned probabilities; the result is called the expected monetary value.

To illustrate the use of these steps, suppose that a Store Manager of Ramson Limited must decide whether to stock Brand A or Brand B. Either brand can be stocked but not both. If A is stocked and it is a success. The manager can make Rs. 200/-, but if it is a failure, there can be a loss of Rs. 500/-. If Brand B is stocked and it is a success, the manager can make Rs. 400/-, but if it is a failure, there can be a loss of Rs. 300/-. Which brand should be stocked? Without some idea of the probabilities of success and failure of these brands, the manager's thinking cannot be quantified. But assume that the manager's feelings about the probabilities of each outcome are shown in Table 5.1

Table 5.1 : Stochastic Table

Probability of	Brand A	Brand B
Success	0.80	0.50
Failure	0.20	0.50

(b) **Payoff Table :** The Store Manager can present the above information in tabular form, showing the conditional values for each strategy (choice of brand) under each state of nature (the combination of uncontrollable factors, such as demand, that determine success or failure). The simplest payoff table as the first step in stating strategies and possible outcomes is shown in Table 5.2.

With the information in Table 5.1 the Store Manager can use subjective estimates of risks assumed above and multiply the conditional values by their probability of occurrence. This calculation will result in expected values. Table 5.2 shows the expected value pay off, using the assumed payoff in Table 5.1 and the above feelings about the probability of success for Brands A and B.

Table 5.2 Payoff Table

Strategy	State of Nature (Demand)	
	Success	Failure
Stock Brand A	Rs. 200/-	Rs. 500/-
Stock Brand B	Rs. 400/-	Rs. 300/-

From the expected value payoff table 5.3, the store manager can determine the total expected value for each strategy by obtaining the sum of the expected values for each state of nature. If Brand A is stocked, the total expected value is Rs. 60/- (Rs. 160-100); if Brand B is stocked, the total expected value is Rs. 50/- (Rs. 200-150); therefore, under the assumptions in this case, the store manager would decide to stock Brand A, because its total expected value is Rs. 10/- more than if Brand B were stocked. Obviously, if the total expected value for stocking each brand had been negative, the manager would decide not to stock either, because there would probably be a loss under either strategy.

Table 5.3 : Expected Value Payoff Table

Strategy	State of Nature	
	Success	Failure

Stock Brand A   Rs. 160/-   Rs. 100/-

Stock Brand B   Rs. 200/-   Rs. 150/-

(c) **Simulation Techniques :** Often, when a management problem is too complex to be answered by series of mathematical equations, it is possible to simulate the probable outcomes before taking action. In this way, the manager may rapidly try out on paper (or with a computer) the results of proposed actions before the actions are taken. By trying out several policies, it is possible to determine which one has the best chance of providing the optimum result.

The idea of randomness represented by random numbers is at the heart of simulation. Random numbers are numbers, each of which has the same chance of being selected. Tables of random numbers are now readily available.

One type of simulation is used in queuing problems, one in which the need for personnel or equipment varies over a time period but the determination of the peak demands cannot be estimated because the occurrence is random or due to chance. With simulation, the manager can try out available strategies as they might result in different outcomes, depending upon probabilities from a table of random numbers. For example, the store manager may wish to determine the work schedules for three sales people to serve customers and to decide whether to add a fourth salesperson. The problem arises from not knowing when customers may appear in the store. Experience may indicate the probabilities that at some hours of the day all three sales people will be serving customers, but that at other times the sales people will be idle. In simulating the traffic for a day, the manager may wish to use subjective probabilities for those times in which there are no data from experience, but even if there are no experience data, it is still possible to simulate an activity by using random numbers.

In practice, simulation is carried out by electronic computers. In seconds, a computer can perform thousands of simulation trails and at the same time compile all costs. At the present time, inventory decision rules are commonly tested on computers. The executive specifies such things as reorder points and order quantity and the computer determines the costs of that policy over the same period of time. After many different policies are put through the series of simulation runs, the best policy can be selected.

(d) **Breakeven Analysis :** The simplest approach for showing the relationship of revenue to cost is the breakeven chart. Revenue and cost can be studied by directing attention to : (i) total revenue and total cost, (ii) average revenue and average cost per unit of output, and (iii) changes in revenue and cost. Breakeven analysis directs attention to the first of these. Breakeven analysis implies that at some point in the operations total revenue equals total cost-the breakeven point. This analysis can be handled algebraically or graphically; however, in all cases, the first step is to classify costs into at least two types-fixed and variable.

The distinction between total fixed and total variable costs stresses that only variable costs will increase with an increase in the production rate of output. However, it should be clear that when average cost per unit is considered, fixed cost per unit of output will decline as volume increases- the constant fixed costs are spread over more units of output. Variable costs per unit of output may increase proportionally with an increase in output , or they may decrease per unit of output (for example, if quantity discounts are significant), or they may increase per unit of output (if the quantity of materials is very short and thus price increases as output increases). In most industries, variable costs per unit can reasonably be assumed to be constant, and thus total variable costs will appear as a straight line (linear) when plotted against various quantities of output. The cost-volume-profit relationship can best be visualized by charting the variables. A breakeven chart is graphical representation of the relationship between costs and revenue at a given time.

The simplest breakeven chart makes use of straight lines that represent revenue, variable costs, and total costs. The construction of this chart requires only that the cost and revenue be known at two points (volumes of output), because only two points are required to draw a straight line. The point at the Y intercept (left hand side of chart) is given by definition : Revenue line will start at zero volume; variable costs also will start at zero volume; fixed costs will be given level on the Y axis because, by definition, they would continue even if there were no production. Cost and revenue data at an actual volume level provide the basis for the necessary second point. All other points on the lines are the results of the assumption of linear relationships for both revenue and costs.

5.7   SUMMARY

Having a logical thought process helps ensure that you will not neglect key factors that could influence the problem, and ultimately your decision. In fact, you should always apply a clear, logical thought process to *all* leadership situations that you encounter. The seven-step process is an excellent tool that can guide you in solving problems and making those sound and timely decisions. The seven steps are: 1. Identify (recognize/define) the problem. 2. Gather information (facts/assumptions). 3. Develop courses of action (solutions). 4. Analyze and compare courses of action (alternatives/solutions). 5. Make a decision; select the best course of action (solution). 6. Make a plan. 7. Implement the plan (assess the results).

In this lesson an attempt has been made to make to understand the importance of decision making in today's context. Decision making has been defined and various characteristics of decision making have also been discussed. The unit dimensional types decision i.e. Organizational vs. Personal, Routine vs. Strategic, Policy vs. Operating, Programmed vs. non Programmed and Individual vs. Group Decision are discussed. Three phases of decision making deal with identification, evaluation and selection of alternative to a problem. The decision making under different conditions has been discussed. Economic man model suggests a logical process of taking decisions, particularly when problem is routine, mechanistic and programmed or when decisions are taken under certainty of conditions.

The decision making process in a group and its difference from individuals decision making is also discussed. The various qualitative techniques : Brainstorming, Synectics, Nominal Grouping; Quantitative Techniques : Stochastic Method, Payoff Table, Decision Tree, Simulation Technique, Break-even Analysis are discussed.

5.8 SELF ASSESSMENT QUESTIONS

1. What is decision-making? What are its basic characteristics?

2. "Decision-making is the primary task of the manager". Discuss and explain the scientific process of decision-making.

3. Explain the various steps in the process of decision-making. Which one is most important and why?

4. What are the principles of decision-making? Design the role of employees' participation in decision-making.

5. Explain the various types of decisions.

6. "Decision-making is the essence of management". Comment.

7. Explain the quantitative techniques of decision-making.

5.9 SUGGESTED READINGS

1. Haynese and Massie, Management Analysis, Concepts and Cases, Prentice Hall of India, New Delhi 1990, p. 147.

2. Harold Koontz and Cyril O. Donnell. Management A Systems and Contingency Analysis of Management Functions, McGraw-Hill Kogakusha Ltd. tokho, 1976 . p. 198.

3. Bass, B.M., Organizational Decision Making. Homewood, III : Richard D. Irwin. Inc.

4. Duncan, J. 1973, Decision Making and Social Issues, Hindale, III : Richard D Irwin. Inc.

5. Maier, N.R.F., 1967. Assets and Liability in group production Solving : The Need for an integrative function. Psychological Review; 4, 239-249.

6. J.R. Bigg, G.N. Plants and L.F. Miller, Dynamics of Participative Groups, M.O. : swift and Co., 1950.

7.

8. Prasad Manmohan, Management Concepts and Practices, Ist edition 1998; Himalaya Publishing House.

www.ingramcontent.com/pod-product-compliance
Lightning Source LLC
Chambersburg PA
CBHW080915170526
45158CB00008B/2118